# BREAKING RANKS®

# 10 Skills
# for Successful
# School Leaders

NATIONAL ASSOCIATION
OF SECONDARY SCHOOL
## PRINCIPALS
Reston, VA

NATIONAL ASSOCIATION
OF SECONDARY SCHOOL
**PRINCIPALS**

1904 Association Drive
Reston, VA 20191-1537
www.principals.org

Steven S. Pophal, *President*
Jana Frieler, *President-Elect*
Gerald N. Tirozzi, *Executive Director*
Lenor G. Hersey, *Deputy Executive Director*
Dick Flanary, *Senior Director of Leadership and Program Services*
Jeanne Leonard, *Senior Director, Marketing, Membership, and Sales*
Robert N. Farrace, *Director of Communications*
John R. Nori, *Director of Program Development*
Pete Reed, *Director of Professional Development*
Patti Kinney, *Associate Director for Middle Level Services*
Mel Riddile, *Associate Director for High School Services*
James Rourke, *Principal Author*
Tanya S. Burke, *Associate Director for Graphic Services*
David Fernandes, *Production Manager*
Jan Umphrey, *Associate Director for Publications*
Sharon Teitlebaum, *Proofreader*
Lisa A. Schnabel, *Graphic Designer*

ISBN 978-0-88210-382-2

# Contents

# Dedication

In 1985, Lenor G. Hersey, deputy executive director, came to NASSP as director of development to work on the Principal's Assessment Center. Since that time, she has played a key role in the creation, design, and delivery of assessment and development activities for aspiring and practicing principals across the country. In addition, her support for the creation of the *Breaking Ranks* series and many other projects has been a major value to NASSP staff and membership.

Without Lenor's work, the content of *10 Skills for Successful School Leaders* would not exist; therefore, the National Association of Secondary School Principals dedicates this work to her with gratitude for her vision, direction, and service.

# Acknowledgements

Nassp would like to thank the thousands of school leaders who have participated in the NASSP Assessment Center process over the last four decades and the following people for their contributions to this guide:

- NASSP staff members Dick Flanary and Pete Reed who have built the assessment and development process upon which this book is based.
- Mel Riddile who first said, "Next we need to write a book about who leads the *Breaking Ranks* change."
- Patti Kinney, John Nori, and Judy Richardson for their writing and critiquing of the drafts.
- Josephine Franklin for her careful updating of and searching for resources.
- Karen Danto and Carolyn Glascock for their constant support of the work.
- Jan Umphrey and Lisa Schnabel for turning a manuscript into a book.
- James R. Rourke, consultant and principal author, for his ability to synthesize the thoughts of so many disparate voices.

In addition, NASSP thanks the principals and others whose voices and writing helped us to illustrate this process: Maria Bradley, Rose Colby, Theresa Hinkle, Ned Kirsch, Stacey Kopnitsky, Janice Koslowski, Ray Landers, Morgan Lee, Delic Loyde, Glenn Pethel, Santo Pino, Mark Wilson, Terry Wolfson, and Edward Yergolanis.

# Who Should Use This Guide and How

Do you look in the mirror before heading out the door to school? Most people who interact with hundreds of people each day typically do—and they adjust their appearance accordingly. If it is so common to look at your outward physical appearance and take into account the perceptions of others, why is it so rare for school leaders to reflect on their practice and what makes them the leaders they are—or should be? No reflection leads to no adjustment. School leaders must feel that they are perfect, right?

Obviously, no principal, assistant principal, or teacher leader would claim perfection. Yet with the improvement of school leadership as their goal, how many school leaders can identify the skills that are required to lead schools in a way that can be assessed and improved upon? Without identifying and reflecting upon those skills, how is it possible to improve practice in any measurable way?

If part of your job is to assess the effectiveness of others based on measurable activities (teacher and student assessment and evaluation, standardized testing, and so on) why shouldn't you expect the same of yourself and why shouldn't others expect it of you? With self reflection, you'll learn what you need to change about yourself to change the outcomes that you get in your school.

For more than three decades, NASSP has been assessing and studying the skills of school leaders. As a result of that experience, an analysis of the principalship, observation, and research, NASSP has identified 10 skills that encompass the bulk of what school leadership entails: setting instructional direction, teamwork, sensitivity, resolving complex problems, judgement, results orientation, organizational ability, oral communication, written communication, developing others, and understanding your own strengths and weaknesses. This guide details those skills and provides discrete, observable, and measurable behaviors.

No time to improve? Conscientious reflection will help you collaborate and delegate more effectively and be more appreciative of the contributions that others can make. Focused practice will enable you to become more effective in certain areas so that you can stop putting out fires (even those that you may have started or contributed to) and start reaping the benefits of collaborative planning. By constructively and systematically asking for focused feedback—in addition to the "how am I doing?" feedback—you can build consensus and culture rather than dissension and controversy. The process of setting instructional direction will eliminate the need to react to unexpected or inferior performance on standardized testing. Better practice will give you more time to do the important work of instructional leadership.

Although skills and behaviors are at the core of this guide, school leaders must develop a base of knowledge through practice as well as through administrator and teacher preparation programs and be morally committed to and inclined to help students learn to the best of their ability. Skills are crucial, but they are of little use without the proper attitude or the underlying knowledge of what school administration and leadership entails. A lack of knowledge or misplaced priorities and attitudes can completely undermine the advantages that are provided by outstanding skills. If you believe in the wrong things, you can be incredibly talented and still take people in the wrong direction.

---

### You Should Take the Path Less Traveled

Regularly reflecting upon and practicing the skills presented in this guide should be the responsibility of all school leaders:

- Veteran principals, assistant principals, and teacher leaders
- Principals who are looking to develop leadership capacity within their staffs
- Mentors of new and aspiring leaders
- New principals
- Aspiring principals and other school leaders
- Principals and other leaders at schools that are not reaching the school's potential.
- University staff members who are charged with preparing principals and teachers.

We ask students to learn for the sake of learning and self-improvement. We assess students in knowledge and the use of skills—and help them to understand their strengths and weaknesses so that together we can work to improve them. Isn't it only fair that school leaders model that behavior in their professional lives?

---

## Ways to Use This Guide

**As an individual.** Every professional assumes final responsibility for his or her own professional development. Although some reliance on others for providing growth experiences is necessary, each person will benefit from reflection on how skills, knowledge, and attitudes in his or her own performance contribute to success or failure of self and the school. Often, we look inward to attribute our success and outward to explain failures. This guide encourages honest reflection and recommends practice of specific behaviors to develop habits that contribute to effective performance.

**To guide a mentor/protégé relationship.** Many successful leaders credit an effective coach or mentor as one important contributor to building the capacity that led to their success. Effective leaders accept coaching for their own development and then develop the capacity to coach and develop others. Developing skills as a focus for coaching has a strong foundation in any activity that requires performance of complex tasks—school leadership is a complex occupation that requires constant integration of a broad set of skills as well as knowledge and dispositions.

**With aspiring leader cohorts or in a principal preparation course.** In asking thousands of school leaders the question, "How did you get to be as good as you are?" NASSP staff members seldom hear a response that indicates that preparation programs and activities have done more than develop a knowledge base. By including the development of essential skills for effective performance, leadership preparation encompasses application, evaluation, and synthesis of knowledge in the context of practice in simulations or on the job.

**To help build individualized developmental activities for an internship.** "What do we want to accomplish during this internship? You have so much to learn and I have so much to teach you." This is often the way that internships work. A more effective model of an internship is one in which the intern has opportunities to apply and practice what has been learned in a real-life context. This requires the incorporation of skill development into the experience.

## Organization of the Guide and Chapters

Chapter 1 provides an overview of the 10 skills, which have been divided into four themes: educational leadership; resolving complex problems; communication; and developing self and others. Each of the remaining chapters (3–6) focuses on the themes and the associated skills and behaviors, as shown in the following illustration:

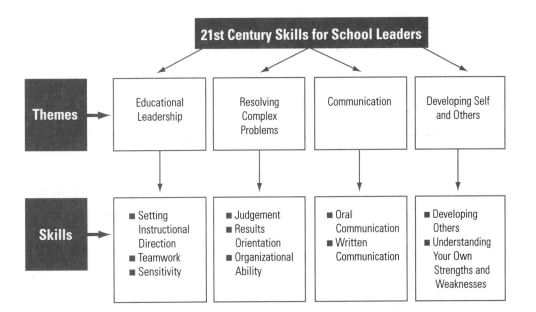

To help you understand the concepts more fully and to conduct that analysis methodically, each skill is divided into four subsections:

- A definition of the term
- Behavioral indicators and descriptors of practice
- Personal development tools and activities that can help you practice the skill to build capacity and effectiveness
- Examples of other school leaders putting the behaviors in action.

## What Will I Take Away From This Guide?

The NASSP assessment and development model has been rigorously tested and refined on the basis of leadership principles and the experience of principals. School leaders using this guide should:

- Understand the skill dimensions that contribute to effective school leadership
- Understand the behaviors that contribute to a high level of performance in each of the skill dimensions
- Understand the skills required to accurately reflect on their own behavior
- Understand how to collect feedback and other data about their own behavior, analyze it, and take action to improve based on the analysis
- Understand how to use the information from their skills diagnosis to construct a professional development plan with goals for development, strategies for finding excellent models, opportunities to practice, methods to obtain constructive feedback, and systems to evaluate progress and revise the plan accordingly.

# 1 Learning and Leading by Example

*The observation of nature is part of an artist's life, it enlarges his form [and] knowledge, keeps him fresh and from working only by formula, and feeds inspiration.*

*—Henry Moore*

Formulas provide the basic tools for modern life. Scientists rely on them for understanding chemical, biological, and physical properties; engineers, programmers, and manufacturers use them as does anyone who uses a recipe to prepare a meal. And yes, schools use them too: best practices, scheduling, teacher to pupil ratios, and so on. Yet too often, we rely only on the formula and forget that it takes more than a plan to implement any practice or make reform work in a specific school context. If a formula were the only thing required, then many of the well-documented best practices should have produced the highest levels of success in every school in the country.

The recent work that NASSP has done in the area of school reform is designed to change the status quo—in the school, in the classroom, and within each school leader. *Breaking Ranks: Changing an American Institution, Breaking Ranks II: Strategies for Leading High School Reform*, and *Breaking Ranks in the Middle: Strategies for Leading Middle Level Reform* each provided recommendations to help schools tackle the "what" of school reform. *Breaking Ranks: A Field Guide for Leading Change* addressed the "how" of fostering change through a process. The goal of this guide is to help each school leader assess his or her knowledge, skills, and dispositions for leading change by examining and practicing 10 leadership skills. Only by doing so can a leader be prepared to take the "what" and the "how" of school change and put them into effective practice so that all students learn and grow.

Every school leader should regularly ask: "What impact do I have on my school's success through my knowledge, skills, and dispositions—not simply through the programs I've helped initiate?" Too often, principals share best practices with colleagues in terms of programs and approaches to leading, but never get around to reflecting on and discussing the personal elements of their success, or their strengths or weaknesses—which more often than not are the very things that enabled a best practice to be successfully adopted; however, even exemplary principals in highly regarded schools often don't understand—or at least can't articulate—how they have personally helped create success.

Is it possible to learn the specific factors related to effective leaders' success? With an often profound lack of self-awareness, how can current school leaders help the next generation of principals to become effective leaders by sharing with them and helping them develop elements of professional performance that contribute to success in school leadership?

How often do you, as a school leader, look at your own behavior or look to develop leadership skills in teacher leaders and your own school leadership team? Too often, we pull a group together for a meeting and call it collaboration. But collaboration happens because of the skills and behaviors of the leader. What skills does he or she bring to the table? Knowledge? Beliefs? Often professional development revolves around increasing knowledge and changing convictions, yet most collaboration breaks down due to inexperience and limited skills or behaviors rather than a lack of knowledge or conviction and motivation.

We must do a better job of understanding that the "what" and "how" of school reform; however, innovation and improvement will struggle to come to fruition without consideration of the personal capacity of the "who" involved in leading the change effort. How often have you heard that the culture of a school wouldn't allow an initiative to be implemented? That the personality of a leader wasn't right for a school? That leadership is innate?

Culture can be changed and leadership skills can be learned. NASSP has engaged in observation, assessment, and development of professional skills to help thousands of school leaders become more effective. Many of those leaders have concrete explanations of what they do and how—answers that can help peers replicate success. Experience and observation have demonstrated that regardless of the point in a school leader's career, he or she should engage in an assessment and development process designed to enhance effective performance. Further, because effective leadership practice is critical to school reform, principals and other school leaders must encourage aspiring leaders and staff members to engage in personal examination and development of their own professional capacity. In doing so, educators grow personally as they contribute to the sustainability of improvements to their schools.

NASSP has studied, refined, and promoted tools that provide individuals with the expertise and wherewithal to become more effective leaders. Those tools, some of which are contained in this guide, are designed to help school leaders develop skills by practicing behaviors, receiving feedback, reflecting, and practicing again. (More extensive tools and activities can be found at www.principals.org as well as through the extensive assessment and development resources, assessment centers, and professional development workshops that are available through NASSP.)

---

## NASSP Assessment and Development

- More than 50 assessment centers (U.S. and international locations)
- In operation for more than three decades
- More than 20,000 prospective and existing leaders trained

## Too Busy to Lead?

If you are too busy to undertake the type of practice and reflection outlined in this guide, then you are too busy to lead. Consider this statement by Edward Yergalonis (2005), a principal with more than 20 years of experience:

> It does not take long for principals to lose their intended focus and settle uncomfortably into the role of operations manager.... Operations management can quickly turn into crisis management. There are days when principals are happy to merely make it through to the end of the day, only to have the vicious cycle begin again the next morning with a new set of operational issues. (p. 40)

Why did you become a teacher, an assistant principal, or a principal? To be a disciplinarian, to help the buses run on time, to chair meetings? Compare what you do on a daily basis with what you would like to do to improve student learning. Are you leading with purpose or allowing daily activities to dictate your personal trajectory—and as a consequence, the trajectory of your school. Without recommitting to your personal mission and continuous self-assessment, you may wake up 30 years into your career and wonder why. Complete the following exercise, and it should soon become clear why it may be time to change your practice.

| Things I Do | Things I Should Do But Don't Have Time | How I Resolve to Address or Things I Shouldn't Do |
|---|---|---|
| • | • | • |

If your daily activities overwhelm strategic planning and school improvement initiatives, then you are not alone. The demands on school leaders at all levels are daunting. Even a cursory review of what principals undertake in an average emergency-free week is instructive. Consider the priorities of a principal juxtaposed against the time spent during a typical day. Many principals report that curricular leadership and establishing a learning climate are among their most important roles, yet they spend more time addressing discipline-related or community and parent issues (see figure 1.1). Time, or the lack thereof, will always be a problem. The question is how are you going to address it?

Figure 1.1

## How Principals Spend Their Time

| Activity | Avg. number of hours per week: All high school principals | Percent indicating "More than 11 hrs/wk": All high school principals | Avg. number of hours per week: Women | Avg. number of hours per week: Men | Avg. number of hours per week: Enrollment 0–599 | Avg. number of hours per week: Enrollment 600–999 | Avg. number of hours per week: Enrollment 1,000–1,999 | Avg. number of hours per week: Enrollment 2000+ |
|---|---|---|---|---|---|---|---|---|
| Dealing with parent issues | 7.64 | 20.9 | 8.39 | 7.48 | 7.43 | 7.54 | 7.98 | 7.93 |
| Discipline | 6.77 | 20.2 | 7.00 | 6.73 | 8.67 | 6.35 | 5.35 | 4.45 |
| Community relations | 6.12 | 14.3 | 6.68 | 5.99 | 5.47 | 6.08 | 6.69 | 7.03 |
| Facilities management | 5.86 | 13.3 | 5.53 | 5.96 | 6.16 | 6.28 | 5.50 | 4.92 |
| Teacher evaluation | 5.15 | 7.9 | 5.80 | 4.98 | 4.77 | 5.27 | 5.46 | 5.48 |
| Program evaluation | 4.85 | 7.2 | 5.40 | 4.72 | 4.48 | 5.20 | 5.01 | 5.16 |
| School safety | 4.64 | 9.3 | 5.30 | 4.49 | 4.28 | 4.66 | 5.02 | 5.03 |
| Curriculum development | 4.35 | 6.2 | 5.29 | 4.12 | 4.22 | 4.52 | 4.37 | 4.29 |
| Budgets | 4.16 | 6.3 | 4.91 | 3.98 | 3.60 | 4.37 | 4.50 | 4.87 |
| Strategic planning | 3.96 | 6.1 | 4.79 | 3.79 | 3.54 | 3.91 | 4.35 | 4.76 |
| Professional development | 3.82 | 4.2 | 4.81 | 3.59 | 3.47 | 3.79 | 4.20 | 4.06 |
| Student assessment | 3.62 | 4.2 | 4.34 | 3.45 | 3.38 | 3.89 | 3.71 | 3.81 |
| Lesson demonstration | 1.26 | 0.7 | 1.44 | 1.23 | 1.30 | 1.27 | 1.22 | 1.25 |
| **Total Average Hours** | **62.21** | | **69.67** | **60.51** | **60.77** | **63.13** | **63.37** | **63.02** |

**Source:** Schiff, T. (2001). Priorities and barriers in high school leadership: A survey of principals. Reston, VA: NASSP.

How will you address the fact that your formal training may not have prepared you completely for the activities you undertake on a daily basis? Effective instructional leadership requires proficiency in strategic planning, student assessment, curriculum development, and program evaluation, yet many principals are neutral about the effectiveness of preservice training in these areas.

So why should a school leader make the time to assess his or her own knowledge, skills and dispositions given the other demands on his or her time? Answers to this question are many:

- More effective leadership fosters improved learning
- More efficient leadership may free-up time
- More focus on a defined framework for self-assessment of strengths and areas of challenge will help prepare a school leader in ways that formal preservice training may not have done.
- Self-assessment and public efforts to improve performance model behavior that every professional in the school community must be engaged in. The only way to improve schools is to increase the capacity of those who work in schools.

Because many principals feel underprepared in specific areas of instructional leadership, such as strategic planning, curriculum development, program evaluation, and student assessment, clearly there is a need for improvement. Your own experience has probably already convinced you of the need to make the time for reflection. The Call to Action exercise that follows should persuade any remaining skeptics. Once the need is clear, a process for self-improvement will be developed in the framework of four primary areas that are important to leadership development:

- Educational leadership
- Resolving complex problems
- Communication
- Developing self and others.

## A Call to Action: What Happens if School Leaders Do Not Assess Their Own Strengths and Weaknesses?

**Q: Why would a seasoned principal or an assistant principal with a lot of classroom experience need to assess his or her strengths and weaknesses?**

**A:** Every school leader needs to know his or her strengths and areas of challenge. By nature, many people who have become principals are confident in their abilities. The reality is, however, that most school leaders and aspiring leaders are strong in one or two of the areas and they lead with those strengths—sometimes exclusively with those strengths. Unfortunately, they may rely on those strengths for everything.

A strength that is overused becomes a weakness. For example, one principal's strength might be sensitivity. The principal always has the pulse of what's going on and the staff loves him or her—until the principal relies exclusively on sensitivity and judgment and decisiveness take a back seat. Another common example is the principal who is very decisive. Decisions are made quickly and decisively, but the decisions may be weak due to a lack of proper analysis or of data or evidence and without sensitive regard for those who will be affected by the decision. Quick decisions are not necessarily good decisions. That kind of principal makes lots of decisions with bad results, which leads to a loss of effectiveness that in turn impacts the school culture. The idea of practicing the skills is to ensure a proper balance in the integration of different skills for the best result.

**Q: What then might a new or aspiring leader learn from these skills that a seasoned leader might already have internalized?**

**A:** Many school leaders come out of the classroom and are strong in certain skills like teamwork, sensitivity, and organizational ability but may be very weak in setting instructional direction, development of others, and written communication—skills that are essential to school leadership. Consequently, long-serving principals may have always relied on those other areas of strength to carry them through. In fact, they may not know what they don't know. The question is whether they have been able to compensate for those initial areas of weakness by understanding and developing them. In addition, if they properly assessed their weaknesses then they may have been able to assemble a team whose strengths complemented their weaknesses. Again, longevity does not necessarily equate to effectiveness in all skill areas. So the message for new leaders with classroom experience is similar: continue to develop those strengths you displayed in the classroom; however, you need to apply them in different and often more complex ways and you need to develop your new skills for use in a broader context than the classroom—the school community.

For example, one English teacher and aspiring principal was shocked to find that his feedback wasn't more glowing in the skill area of written communication. Certainly his grammar and prose were acceptable. But his writing was not as effective as it could have been for the job of the principal—a different kind of writing for a different kind of job, a different audience, and a different purpose.

**Q: What is a distinguishing benefit of assessment?**

**A:** Feedback. School leaders become numb to praise, criticism, and blame and the regular struggle of who to listen to on any given topic. A genuine and thoughtful assessment process is an opportunity for growth rather than an evaluation process or other exchanges that have an opportunity to become adversarial. If you want to become a better leader, external feedback is critical. You have to understand how you measure up against certain skill sets—not only in your own eyes but also in the eyes of others. You can't develop yourself unless you're aware of how others see you. Visualize the Johari Window—a four-pane window, with each pane representing a different view: the traits that the participant and peers see (arena); the things that the participant sees but the peers do not (façade); the things that the peers see but the participant does not (blind spot), and the behaviors or motives that were not ascribed to the participant by anyone. It is important to understand and appreciate the importance of each of these panes or perspectives. Developing a systematic process to gather those perspectives will ensure the most favorable results. The more organized your feedback process and the wider the net you cast for feedback, the more potential there is for professional growth.

**Q: What happens when a school leader doesn't examine his or her own strengths and weaknesses?**

**A:** Unconscious incompetence. It may sound harsh, but that's the reality. It is possible, but highly unlikely that a principal can be good in all these skills without extensive awareness and practice. Unfortunately, that could mean muddling along (unconsciously) with a level of competence veiled in good intentions that does nothing to improve student learning within the school. More concretely, schools in which leaders don't set the instructional direction have everyone doing their own thing with haphazard results; where teamwork is missing, hierarchical top-down decision making takes place; where sensitivity reins supreme at the expense of other skills, the principal is always running around trying to make up for bad decisions; where judgment and analysis are lacking, the principal shoots from the hip; where the principal has not made a concerted effort to develop others, a sense of dependency takes over and the staff can't function when the principal leaves the building—even for the day. The skills for leadership require a complex balancing act—one that takes practice and motivation. If you don't have the right motivation, then the skills don't matter: you have to believe in people and have a sincere desire to move things forward.

**Q: What stands out to you about the 10 skills?**

**A:** They are based on common sense. Many people look at the skills and say "oh, that's easy" or "I am effective with all of those." In truth, there is very little that is earth shattering about the skills. Yet what we find time and again is that even if people understand the general skills they rarely integrate them into their practice. They rely on just a couple of the skills. Further, if they took the time to ask peers to assess them on these "simple" skills, the peers might offer a very different perspective. The assessment and development process that is outlined in this book allows for an objective assessment and an opportunity to grow. Perhaps more important than the skills are the behavioral indicators—the "look-fors"—and most practitioners can't readily point these out. The indicators are things that principals can actually practice to improve the overall skill sets. (The indicators are discussed in detail in chapters 3–6.)

**Q: What kind of leader would find the skill areas covered in this book most helpful?**

**A:** Every school leader or aspiring school leader needs to regularly assess their strengths and weaknesses and develop a plan to address them. Others who may benefit include:

- Experienced principals and assistant principals who want to re-dedicate themselves to becoming more effective leaders—especially in the area of instructional leadership.

- Principals who want to use it as a guide to cultivate and mentor assistant principals, teacher leaders, and other leaders within their own schools.

- Aspiring principals.

**Q: How do these skills relate to leadership standards?**

**A:** They are the components that can be developed. Look at the Educational Leadership Policy Standards: ISLLC 2008 (see Appendix 1) they are extremely complex—similar in complexity to many of the existing state learning standards. Meeting the standards requires breaking them up into component parts. It would be far too difficult to simply "practice" a standard, yet by practicing various behaviors you can meet the standard. (See Appendix 1 for an activity to assist you in unpacking the standards and skills and better understanding the relationship between the two.)

**Q: What's Next?**

**A:** Developing the skills and behaviors described in this guide. Too often, it is only the aspiring or new principal or assistant principal who feels the need to practice and perfect each of these areas. As one might expect, there are different levels of attainment on the route to theoretical perfection. The NASSP tools (the Assessment Center and the online assessment at www .principals.org) help leaders to improve in each of the skill areas and to become more capable leaders. Practice, attainment, and exhibition of the skills can then be compared against certain standards for leadership, such as the Educational Leadership Policy Standards ISLLC 2008, to help gauge the effectiveness of school leaders.

NASSP has been working with the National Board for Professional Teaching Standards (NBPTS) to help recognize school leader effectiveness much the same way that NBPTS has done for board certified teachers. That collaboration has resulted in the National Board Certification for Educational Leaders. Under the new Core Propositions for Accomplished Educational Leaders (Appendix XX), NBPTS would tentatively offer these new certifications:

- National Board Certification for Principals

- National Board Certification for Assistant Principals

- National Board Certification for Teacher Leaders

Reflecting upon your own practice and understanding and internalizing the skills contained in this guide will be a major step forward for you professionally and personally—regardless of whether or not you strive for advanced certification.

***Source:*** *Excerpts from a conversation with NASSP assessment and development staff, August 12, 2009.*

**Reference**

Yergolanis, E. (2005). A principal's journey [Middle Level Edition]. *Principal Leadership, 6*(4), pp. 40–43.

# 2 21st Century Principal Skills and Your Process for Improvement

*We need to prepare ourselves for the possibility that sometimes big changes follow from small events, and that sometimes these changes can happen very quickly.*

—*Malcolm Gladwell,* The Tipping Point

NASSP offers an assessment and development framework around four themes:

- Educational leadership
- Resolving complex problems
- Communication skills
- Developing self and others.

Within these four themes are 10 primary skill areas to assess and develop. Collectively, these skills are referred to as the NASSP 21st Century Principal Skill Dimensions (see figure 2.1). The skills are also aligned with the Educational Leadership Policy Standards: ISLLC 2008 (see Appendix 1 for the standards).

---

Figure 2.1
**21st Century Principal Skills**

**Educational Leadership**

- **Setting instructional direction.** Implementing strategies for improving teaching and learning including putting programs and improvement efforts into action. Developing a vision of learning and establishing clear goals; providing direction in achieving stated goals; encouraging others to contribute to goal achievement; securing commitment to a course of action from individuals and groups.

- **Teamwork.** Seeking and encouraging involvement of team members. Modeling and encouraging the behaviors that move the group to task completion. Supporting group accomplishment.

- **Sensitivity.** Perceiving the needs and concerns of others; dealing tactfully with others in emotionally stressful situations or in conflict. Knowing what information to communicate and to whom. Relating to people of varying ethnic, cultural, and religious backgrounds.

---

### Resolving Complex Problems

- **Judgment.** Ability to make high quality decisions based on data; skill in identifying educational needs and setting priorities; assigning appropriate priority to issues; and in exercising caution. Ability to seek, analyze, and interpret relevant data.

- **Results orientation.** Assuming responsibility. Recognizing when a decision is required. Taking prompt action based on data as issues emerge. Resolving short-term issues while balancing them against long-term objectives.

- **Organizational ability.** Planning and scheduling one's own and the work of others so that resources are used appropriately. Scheduling flow of activities; establishing procedures to monitor projects. Practicing time and task management; knowing what to delegate and to whom.

### Communication

- **Oral communication.** Clearly communicating. Making oral presentations that are clear and easy to understand.

- **Written communication.** Ability to express ideas clearly and correctly in writing; to write appropriately for different audiences—students, teachers, parents, and others.

### Developing Self and Others

- **Developing others.** Teaching, coaching, and helping others. Providing specific feedback based on observations and data.

- **Understanding own strengths and weaknesses.** Identifying personal strengths and weaknesses. Taking responsibility for improvement by actively pursuing developmental activities. Striving for continuous learning.

Developing excellence in any endeavor requires breaking the broad task into its component parts, practicing each part, receiving feedback on performance, adjusting practice on the basis of feedback, and eventually integrating all of the components to perform the broader task. The skill dimensions are component parts of the broader task of effective school leadership. Each of the 10 skill dimensions is broken down into specific behavioral indicators or descriptors of practice in the remaining chapters [to review a combined list of skills and indicators, see Appendix 3].

These are skills that a school leader reading this guide may choose to focus on and find opportunities for practice and feedback. However, before selecting areas of focus for professional development, school leaders and aspiring leaders must first assess their strengths. Too often educators use the "deficit model" to guide their development. But participants in NASSP assessments focus on their areas of strength first to reinforce the idea that school leaders should practice and build on strengths rather than only on improving weaknesses.

Certainly there are weaknesses that can derail your career; however, most weaknesses can be eliminated or managed with proper and sustained development through collaboration with others who have strengths in your areas of weakness. This can only

> **Term Primer**
>
> **Knowledge:** What one knows
>
> **Skills:** What one can do
>
> **How are "knowledge" and "skills" related?** Aeronautical engineers probably "know" a great deal more about how planes fly than pilots know. With whom would you rather fly, an experienced pilot or an aeronautical engineer?
>
> **Dispositions:** Who one is and what one believes (includes personal traits and characteristics)
>
> **Habits:** Behaviors that result from repeated and successful use of behavioral indicators associated with skills.

occur with accurate self-knowledge and application of specific strategies to diminish the weaknesses' impact on professional performance. You must know your strengths and build upon them to ameliorate some of your deficits.

## How Are Skills and Behavior Related?

Skill manifests itself through behavior—usually complex behavior appropriately applied in the context of a specific situation. Each of the skill dimensions relies on demonstrations of specific behavior for diagnosis of strength or weakness and for further development. Specific behavioral indicators further define each skill dimension. Each skill dimension has its own unique descriptors of practice; to illustrate, the behavioral indicators for setting instructional direction are:

- Articulates a vision related to teaching and learning
- Articulates high performance expectations for self or others
- Encourages improvement in teaching and learning
- Sets clear measurable objectives
- Generates enthusiasm toward common goals
- Seeks to develop alliances outside the school to support high-quality teaching and learning
- Acknowledges achievement or accomplishments
- Seeks commitment to a course of action.

The indicators provide actions that can be practiced and refined. A colleague or a coach can observe them and provide behaviorally specific feedback regarding the level of effectiveness demonstrated during practice and performance. Behavioral indicators can become the focus of purposeful and intentional practice that takes place in the context of the job setting. Without indicators or descriptors, it becomes difficult if not impossible to gauge one's effectiveness. In subsequent chapters, you will find the descriptors for each of the 10 skills; however, the "setting instructional direction" skill will be used as an example for the remainder of this chapter to illustrate how to develop a plan to address all 10 skills.

## The Process Delineated

Despite all of the challenges that school leaders face, many continue to be inspirational forces within schools. How can they help themselves become even more effective and efficient? *Breaking Ranks: A Field Guide for Leading Change* provided the "process circle" (see figure 2.2) to use in the pursuit of school improvement. At the heart of any school improvement initiative, however, lies a focus on individual development for every member of your team. The same process can guide the analysis and assessment of leaders' needs and strengths. The principal should be the model and driving force behind administrator and teacher self- and peer-assessment and development.

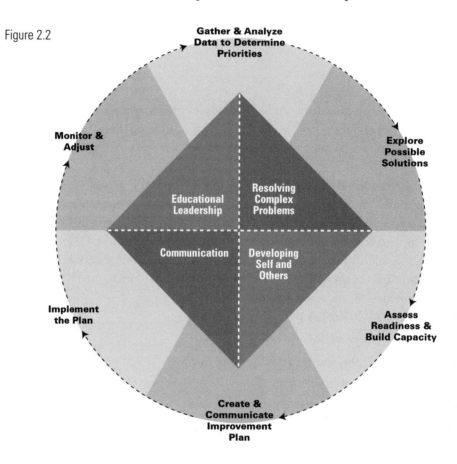

Figure 2.2

Gather & Analyze Data to Determine Priorities

Explore Possible Solutions

Monitor & Adjust

Resolving Complex Problems

Educational Leadership

Communication

Developing Self and Others

Implement the Plan

Assess Readiness & Build Capacity

Create & Communicate Improvement Plan

Although a school's learning trajectory will never be onward and upward without a skilled principal and leadership team, leaders should nevertheless be careful to distinguish between their own professional development plans and their school's plan for improvement. The needs of the school should obviously inform the unique professional development needs of each person who works in the school. Individual professional development plans are designed to build capacity to perform in support of the school improvement plan.

Each section of the chart on page 14 mirrors a section of the process circle. We have completed the chart using "setting instructional direction" as an example. In subsequent chapters, you will be asked to complete the chart as it relates to the specific skill you want to work on given your own circumstances. Refer to this chart for ideas and be certain to know the descriptors of practice and behaviors for each skill so that you

*10 Skills for Successful School Leaders*

understand what data is required. For example, here again are the descriptors for setting instructional direction:

- Articulates a vision related to teaching and learning
- Articulates high performance expectations for self or others
- Encourages improvement in teaching and learning
- Sets clear measurable objectives
- Generates enthusiasm toward common goals
- Seeks to develop alliances outside the school to support high quality teaching and learning
- Acknowledges achievement or accomplishments
- Seeks commitment to a course of action.

In the remaining chapters you will be asked to complete your own chart for each skill. To reinforce the point that assessment and development should be a continuous process, at the end of each chart, you will be instructed to return to the "Gather & Analyze Data" step to establish new priorities either within the same skill or to begin work on another skill.

Improvement is incremental and therefore requires you to continually adjust and reset your priorities and goals on the basis of monitoring. Sometimes that will mean that you are satisfied that your practice in a skill is just enough to get you where you want to be for the moment and instead need to address another skill. At other times, monitoring may point you in the direction of continuing to practice certain behaviors or to set new priorities within the same skill.

As you complete the chart for each skill area, you will begin to realize that the following developmental components appear repeatedly:

- Mentoring, coaching, and reflection
- Simulations and practice
- Feedback.

Because these components are so important to developing skills through practice, they are discussed in detail in the next several pages. By reviewing them, you should be able to complete the skill activities charts with a more complete understanding of your options and create a richer development plan.

| Process Circle Step | How Do *You* Put the Skill Into Action? (e.g., setting instructional direction) |
| --- | --- |
| **Gather & Analyze Data** | **Ask:** How is my on-the-job performance in this skill area? |

**Gather & Analyze Data**

**Ask:** How is my on-the-job performance in this skill area?

■ Reflect on my performance of the "setting instructional direction" behavioral indicators—the frequency of my engaging in each behavior as opposed to my ability to perform the behavior.

■ Solicit face-to-face feedback from a variety of sources—such as a mentor, a coach, a supervisor, supervisees, and colleagues—that focuses on the setting instructional direction indicators.

■ Seek anonymous feedback from the 360-degree tool available from NASSP (www.principals.org).

■ Seek data from a formal assessment process (e.g., Selecting and Developing 21st Century Leaders or Leadership Skills Assessments from NASSP).

■ Review how I measure my performance on the indicators. Discuss results with mentor or colleague.

**Possible Solutions & Strategies**

Assignments that stretch and provide practice in this skill:

■ Accept leadership of an ad hoc group with a difficult task, a group of inexperienced or unskilled people, or a loosely structured group to practice bringing structure and direction to a group in order to accomplish tasks.

■ Convene a committee or task force to study an issue regarding teaching and learning. Use a written charge that you have drafted for that group. In that charge, include the specific purpose and objectives for the group related to improved learning, the advisory or decision-making status of the group, resources that are available to assist in the group's work, to whom the group will report, your expectations, and deadlines or a timeline.

■ Meet regularly with staff members to discuss their priorities. Provide input on the basis of your expectations as an instructional leader in the organization.

■ Study group dynamics in actual work groups and identify the behaviors that assist and hinder the groups in completing their tasks.

■ Seek opportunities to chair problem-solving committees at the school or district level. Ask a mentor or colleague to monitor progress and provide feedback regarding effective use of planning skills and follow-through.

■ Organize your faculty into focus groups. Form a cadre to train aspiring leaders within your own school or district and lead this group yourself.

**Workshops, seminars, and courses**

■ Check your district, regional service agency, state department, or colleges and universities in your area for opportunities for building capacity in this skill area.

■ Participate in seminars dealing with effective management, administrative effectiveness, and conducting effective meetings.

**Mentor, coaches, and supervisors**

■ Develop a mentor relationship with a colleague who can provide guidance in identifying critical instructional leadership and school management issues and in assigning appropriate priority to these issues.

| Process Circle Step | How Do *You* Put the Skill Into Action? (e.g., setting instructional direction) |
|---|---|
| **Possible Solutions & Strategies** | ■ Discuss with a mentor actual school issues focusing on the effective school leader's use of skills in judgment and results orientation to set high priorities for instructional leadership and the management of learning.<br><br>**Readings**<br><br>■ Bennis, W.. *On becoming a leader: The leadership classic.* (2009). Revised and Updated. Philadelphia, PA: Basic Books,<br><br>■ Blanchard, K., Carew, D., and Parisi-Carew, E. (2009). *The one minute manager builds high performing teams: Excellence through team building.* New York, NY: William Morrow,.<br><br>■ Blasé, J. J. and Kirby, P. C. (2000). *Bringing out the best in teachers: What effective principals do.* Second Edition. Thousand Oaks, CA: Corwin Press,<br><br>■ Carnegie, D. & Associates, Inc. (2001). *The leader in you: How to win friends, influence people, and succeed in a changing world.* New York, NY: Simon & Schuster.<br><br>**Off-the-job development opportunities**<br><br>■ Become active in community and professional organizations. Seek leadership roles within committees in these organizations.<br><br>■ Participate in a district-level or state-level seminar or graduate course in group dynamics or interpersonal communications.<br><br>**NASSP professional development opportunities**<br>■ Online courses<br>■ Seminars<br>■ Web-based resources<br>■ Customized professional development<br>(Visit www.principals.org/ProfessionalDevelopment.aspx to see current offerings.) |
| **Assess Readiness & Build Capacity** | ■ Review the possible solutions in light of school data that has implications for my professional development needs: achievement; instructional staff members' qualifications, experience, background, and so on; student, staff member, and school community demographics; attendance; drop-out rate; graduation rate and so on.<br><br>■ **Ask:** What development can I engage in that will have the greatest impact on my personal/professional capacity and the needs of the school?<br><br>■ Consider how specific personal development activities will affect others with whom you work. |
| **Create & Communicate Plan** | ■ Develop a personal learning plan (PLP) that delineates how you will practice this skill, your development activities, and your goals (See Chapter 7 to create a PLP).<br><br>■ Be an example of a "head learner" by sharing your PLP with others and encouraging every adult in the building to have a learning plan that is based on their developmental needs in the context of the needs of the school and the students. |
| **Implement Plan** | ■ Practice the indicators to build capacity in the skill: implement the strategies selected from possible solutions. |

| Process Circle Step | How Do *You* Put Skill Into Action? (e.g., setting instructional direction) |
|---|---|
| **Monitor & Adjust** | ■ Take continuous measures of your progress and the impact of your progress on the needs of your school as you practice. |
| | ■ Refer to the data sources you used in collecting the original data that formed the basis of your development plan (PLP). |
| | ■ Seek feedback from colleagues, peers, mentors, supervisors—and remember the PLP is public! |
| | ■ Reflect |
| | ■ Keep a Journal |
| | ■ Return to "Gather & Analyze Data" to establish new priorities with the same skill or to begin work on another skill. |

## Know Where You Are: Resources to Get Started

NASSP has developed a variety of resources for personal assessment and development. Some of them are contained in this guide. You may want to take the online assessment (available at www.principals.org), which will provide you with anonymous feedback, or attend an NASSP Assessment Center. The online assessment will help you determine weaknesses, strengths, and priorities and will provide some feedback and can be used to complement this guide. This assessment seeks to diagnose your capacity to perform, practice in the context of your work setting, and build strengths in the 10 skill dimensions that contribute to success in leading elementary, middle level, or high schools.

The online version of the NASSP Leadership Skills Assessment is a five-step assessment:

1. **Explore the skills dimensions.** You will examine your interest in developing specific skills that have proven to be essential to effective school leadership. During this process, you will learn about 10 crucial skill dimensions and specific behavioral indicators that contribute to building skill in each dimension.

2. **Complete a 360-degree assessment.** You will assess your own practice of these same skills and invite up to 15 colleagues to assess your practice so that you may compare how others perceive your performance with your own perceptions. The purpose of the 360-degree tool is to help determine the behaviors you exhibit as a part of your typical response to most situations you deal with. When people are under pressure, they resort to the behaviors or habits that have served them well, that have gotten them where they are. When you consider the frequency with which you engage in each of the behaviors in the assessment, participants think of the habits and the behaviors that are most frequently part of their initial response to situations.

3. **In-basket activity.** Your responses to a variety of issues that school leaders typically face will be used to assess your performance in the skill dimensions during the in-basket activity. You may assess your own performance and have the opportunity to request that two colleagues assess your performance as demonstrated in your in-basket responses. (See Appendix 4 for sample in-basket activities.)

4. **Reports.** When you complete the activities described above, you may view and print a report for each. When you have completed all of the assessment activities, you may view and print a summary report that pulls together data from all three of these sources. This report ranks the skills listed above in terms of your developmental interests and level of skill demonstrated.

5. **Development plan.** After reviewing the data in your summary report, you will decide which skills you want to develop first and which types of professional development strategies work best for you. Based on these decisions, the final report will provide you with specific developmental strategies and a development guide for building an individualized personal learning plan. (See Chapter 7)

## Mentoring and Coaching

A mentor is an experienced role model who guides the professional development of a less experienced protégé through coaching. Both the mentor and the protégé learn about themselves, improve their skills, and grow professionally.

Coaching is the process used by the mentor as he or she works with the protégé to examine the behavior of the protégé for the purpose of gaining insights that lead to improved performance. Coaching involves the skills of observing and recording behavior, giving feedback, asking probing questions that enhance reflection, listening, analyzing behavior as it relates to professional skill, and knowledge.

### Benefits of Seeking and Using a Mentor
### For you as the protégé

- Expanded knowledge of leadership skills and management practices
- Increased access to challenging opportunities and responsibilities
- Development of an administrative perspective
- Association with a successful role model
- Opportunity to discuss administrative and educational issues with a respected practitioner
- Ongoing support and encouragement
- Honest and constructive feedback
- Access to inside information and organization dynamics
- Help in building a professional network
- Increased self-confidence—heightened career aspirations

### For your mentor

- Recognition as a successful administrator
- Increased feeling of self-worth from contributing to education and the organization
- Opportunity to reflect on own skills and practices
- Exposure to fresh ideas
- Added incentive for staying current in the field
- Personal satisfaction in teaching and sharing experience
- Sense of pride in protégé's accomplishments

**For your school or district**

- Increases administrator talent pool
- Expands the knowledge base and skill level of potential principals and practicing principals
- Builds morale of protégés and mentors
- Fosters increased administrator productivity and effectiveness
- Reduces administrator turnover
- Promotes more administrative continuity in system
- Provides cost-effective development experiences for aspiring administrators
- Improves quality of school leadership
- Creates better working environment for teachers
- Enhances learning environment for students

**Mentor Functions**

- Mentors foster your belief in yourself
- Mentors teach and model specific skills
- Mentors challenge and empower
- Mentors provide feedback and foster reflection
- Mentors help in development of a broader perspective
- Mentors encourage professional growth through reading, professional associations, and academic coursework
- Mentors provide insight into the social and political mores of the profession and the organization
- Mentors help the protégé build a professional network
- Mentors are available
- Mentors provide support and encouragement
- Mentors are role models
- Mentors share knowledge and information

**Mentor Qualifications**
**In selecting someone to serve as your mentor, consider someone who:**

- Has confidence in his/her own personal and professional development
- Enjoys giving support and encouragement to colleagues and protégés on a one-to-one basis
- Has a personal reputation as an experienced effective school leader
- Is knowledgeable about current educational issues and practices
- Has sufficient experience to be knowledgeable about schools and school systems
- Possesses an understanding of political and organizational dynamics in relation to education
- Has an understanding of specific leadership and management skills and the key behaviors relative to them
- Is committed to the mentoring process
- Has made the necessary arrangements to have time available to work with a protégé over an extended period of time
- Does not have any current supervisory or evaluation role in relation to the protégé

- Is open to new ideas
- Is sensitive to the needs and concerns of others
- Practices effective listening skills
- Presents a professional demeanor
- Has received special mentor training.

**In your first meeting with your mentor seek to establish a relationship that will foster your professional growth. Some of the following activities are appropriate for your first conversations:**

- Sharing professional background information
- Discussing mentor/protégé expectations
- Identifying your areas of strength and needs for improvement
- Establishing your developmental goals and objectives
- Designing your individual professional development plan
- Discussing potential development opportunities.

**As you begin to carry out the activities in your professional development plan, you should expect your mentor to engage in some of the following activities:**

- Observing your behavior in specific situations as requested by you
- Listening to your analysis of your concerns and behaviors as they relate to the skills and knowledge you seek to develop
- Giving you behaviorally specific feedback
- Reinforcing your effective performances and achievements with behaviorally specific feedback
- Helping you explore strategies for building on the strengths you consistently demonstrate
- Helping you explore strategies for refining performances and behaviors that are not as effective as you would like
- Sharing with you understanding of education organization structures and cultures
- Introducing you to other experienced administrators who might serve as mentors to you in their own areas of expertise and experience.

## Feedback

Feedback is a powerful tool for growth and development. After observing your performance, you and the mentor meet for a feedback session to discuss what happened during the observation. The mentor facilitates the feedback session by asking questions that prompt you to reflect on the experience and to analyze personal performance. The mentor should also share observations and analysis of your performance in a non-threatening manner. The mentor will use the skills of listening, questioning, and summarizing. The feedback is used to plan the next steps for your professional development.

Reflective review and coaching are used when the mentor cannot observe your behavior or performance firsthand. This approach requires that you record and analyze your own behavior for improved performance. In a meeting with you after the event or incident, your mentor can assist you in further analysis of your performance. Working together, you and your mentor explore ways to improve your performance. The key skills used by the mentor in this coaching activity are listening, questioning, and sensitivity.

## Practice Makes Perfect

Even with practice, perfection is a tall order. Practicing in a simulation does, however, allow you to test your skills without some of the ramifications of on-the-job mistakes. Other than a fire drill, when was the last time you simulated handling a work-related issue involving peers? Much of the assessment work done by NASSP revolves around simulations of school-related activities. Those activities often help in the selection of school leaders. They are also extremely beneficial in helping experienced principals understand their strengths and weaknesses.

Simulations:

- Provide a low threat environment in which to practice and learn the process for on-the-job development of specific skills.
- Provide structured opportunities for learning the skills and indicators more fully.
- Remove the possibility of negative ramifications for mistakes and errors in judgment made during practice.
- Remove emotional ties that may be attached to real-life situations.
- Create opportunities for receiving immediate feedback about performance and effectiveness from observers.
- Open opportunities for dialogue that is not fettered by confidentiality concerns that may exist around real-life situations.

Two sample simulations follow. The first can be done with a colleague and another observer and the second can be used in a group setting. Each scenario typically requires a performer, at least one responder, and at least one observer. Colleagues who are serving as observers expand their knowledge and understanding of behaviors and strategies that contribute to effective performance in a variety of situations. Responders learn how it feels to be on the "other side of the desk" from the principal. The content of these learning and practice activities gives participants opportunities to practice specific behavioral indicators as well as to become familiar with realistic situations that they, in all probability, will encounter as they serve as school leaders. In some of the simulations, you will need to use a role-player (responder) to establish the context for the issue; however, the individual who is practicing the skill development should not play any role other than him- or herself within the context of the particulars given about the situation.

## Directions for Performer

(In the first scenario the performer is the principal.)

- Read the scenario: 2–5 minutes
- Review the skills and indicators and decide which skill dimensions and indicators you will focus on for practice in this scenario. Relate these to the observer and responder.
- Lead or conduct the meeting with the responder.
- Participate in the feedback loop led by the observer.

During the feedback loop, the performer will:

- Reflect on his or her performance as it relates to the key behavioral indicators that were the focus of the simulation.
- State the indicators that were demonstrated particularly well during the scenario.
- State what would be done differently if he or she could perform the scenario again immediately.
- Listen to the feedback from the responder.
- Listen to the feedback from the observer.

## Directions for Responder

(In the first scenario, the responder is Pat Strickler, a social studies teacher and the chairperson of a newly forming committee).

- Read the performer's scenario.
- If there is a section for the responder to guide your action during the scenario, read that information and decide how to play the role called for in the scenario.
- Participate with the performer. Be cooperative and follow his or her lead in the meeting. Respond in the way that you think the person in the scenario would if this were a real-life situation.
- Participate in the feedback loop as led by the observer.

When the responder gives feedback to the performer you will:

- Listen to the performer share reflections of his or her performance.
- Tell the performer three indicators or skills that he or she demonstrated particularly well. Focus on the skills that were identified for focus.

- Make a suggestion for an improvement that the performer might make to enhance effectiveness.
- Listen to the observer as he or she gives feedback to the performer.

**Directions for Observer**

Record the performer's behavior during the interaction. Record the performer's reflections and feedback given during the feedback loop. Optional: Videotape the performance and feedback.

Keep the following schedule:
- 2–5 minutes: Everyone reads the performer's scenario
- 5 minutes: Performer decides which skill dimensions and indicators he or she will focus on for the scenario and relates these to the observer and responder.
- 10–15 minutes: Performer leads or conducts the meeting with the person who is not the observer in this round (the responder).
- 15 minutes: Feedback given.

Facilitate the feedback loop by:
A. Starting with the performer, ask the following questions (remember to record or take notes):
  - What did you do particularly well as it relates to the key behavioral indicators on which you were focusing during this simulation?
  - What would you do differently if you could perform the simulation all over again right now?
B. Ask the responder to give feedback to the performer:
  - What did the performer do particularly well as it relates to the key behaviors he or she identified for focus? What improvements might be made?
  - Keep the ratio at three positive skill demonstrations to one suggestion for improvement. Focus on building strengths.
C. As the observer, you speak last to:
  - Add new points that have not been discussed
  - Encourage the performer to view the videotape
  - Distribute feedback and reflection sheets to the performer.
D. If the interaction was recorded, give the disk or tape to the performer. If not, give the performer your notes regarding his or her performance and feedback.

## Scenario 1

(One-on-one + observer)
Accreditation Visit—Jefferson High School

You are the principal of Jefferson High School. The school will soon be going through an accreditation by the Regional Association of Colleges and Schools. This will be the first time for Jefferson. Other high schools in the district are already members, but Jefferson, being relatively new, has not gone through the process yet. The board of education and the superintendent, however, have decided it's time for your school to become accredited.

Your responsibility is to see that the procedures, as spelled out by the accrediting association, are followed. The main components include a school self-evaluation and a visit by an accreditation team.

One of your first acts was to name a steering committee of staff members to work on this effort. Out of a total faculty and staff of 60 people, 5 have volunteered to serve initially, with 8 more ready to join the committee at the proper time. Pat Strickler, a social studies teacher, has agreed to be the chairperson. You are meeting with Pat in your office after school to plan the activities necessary to comply with the requirements of the accreditation process.

How will you proceed?

## Scenario 2

(Group simulation)

Teacher Evaluation—Northeast Middle School

As principal of Northeast Middle School, you are concerned about the teacher evaluation procedure that is being used at the school. A conversation with science teacher Leslie Hines reinforced your worry. Leslie was referred to you for some alleged deficiencies. You were concerned about how best to evaluate Leslie for both summative and formative purposes. You found the present system to be of no help.

You have decided to form a committee of Northeast faculty members to help you start from scratch in formulating an evaluation procedure to effectively diagnose teachers' strengths and identify areas for improvement. You are interested in a system that can be used to determine whether a teacher is to be given tenure, but the major thrust of any exceptional system is to help teachers grow professionally. Observation instruments are needed to support the evaluation procedure.

A committee composed of your assistant principal, a guidance counselor, the teachers association building representative, and two team leaders are meeting with you after school in the conference room to talk about a new evaluation process that ultimately will be used to advise the district level evaluation committee.

Conduct the meeting.

## Feedback Loop

Once the simulation has concluded, feedback begins. Key elements of the feedback include:

- Observer facilitates
- The performer reflects on his or her performance and states three examples of effective performance and one thing that he or she would do differently.
- The responder provides feedback regarding three effective demonstrations of skill and makes one suggestion for improved performance. The feedback should focus first on the skills selected by the performer. They may also include skills from other areas if they were particularly strong or particularly weak.
- The observer gives feedback to fill in the blanks using the notes made during the performance to substantiate. The observer might note, for example, that when the performer said, "I need to know what you think and how you feel about this issue," it was a strong example of the sensitivity indicator, eliciting the feelings, needs, and concerns of others.

- Keep the ratio of three positives to one suggestion. Frequently, the performer will start with the things that he or she did not perform well. Stop them by saying, "Time out. Start with the things you believe you did well." Try to give as much time to each of the behaviors performed well as to the behavior not performed well.
- Feedback is a gift. When we receive it, we should say only, "Thank you." There is no need for the performer to justify, explain, rationalize, or defend behavior or performance. This takes time and is not productive.
- The gift of feedback should generate reflection. The recipient should "try it on" to see how it fits. As with other gifts, some will be more valuable than others. Honestly reflecting on the feedback to determine its value is an important step in using the information to guide efforts to improve performance.

# 3 Educational Leadership

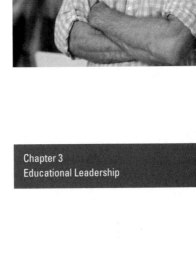

*Mountaintops inspire leaders but valleys mature them.*

—*Winston Churchill*

## Setting Instructional Direction ■ Teamwork ■ Sensitivity

Increased accountability for every student's learning, a changing world driven by technological innovation and complexity, and greater diversity of school communities have created a sense of urgency for school leaders. This confluence of events has signaled the end of equating a school's level of activity with its level of success—necessitating a shift in focus from process to outcomes (see Figure 3.1). Finding and preparing effective school leaders has never been more important. NASSP has more than three decades of experience in assessing the skills of school leaders and now those attributes are also perceived as crucial by a greater portion of the educational community. When schools became accountable for each student's success, instructional leadership skills take precedence over administrative skills.

Figure 3.1
**A Shift in Focus**

| Old school | New school |
|---|---|
| Managers | Instructional leaders |
| Adult-focused | Student-focused |
| Learning time is a constant | Learning time is a variable |
| Teaching | Learning |
| Seat time | Mastery |
| Bell curve | J curve |
| Covering content | Mastering essential learning |
| Access for all | Excellence for all |
| Success for some | Success for all |
| Individual star teachers | Teams |
| Status Quo | Change |

Engaging in *Breaking Ranks* reform requires decisive action to improve teaching and learning. Creating an environment that produces results while respecting the professionals and students who are involved in the process is the essence of educational leadership. Decisive action includes establishing clear and measurable goals, providing direction, involving others, and securing commitment. Tact, effective communication, and interpersonal relations are important. Remember, the greatest vision or goal accompanied by little tact and ineffective communication can become a nightmare. The following section examines three key skill dimensions of educational leadership: setting instructional direction, teamwork, and sensitivity.

## Behaviors Associated with Educational Leadership

School leaders' responsibility for the formation and communication of the school's vision and direction is the first item under Collaborative Leadership in the *Breaking Ranks* Venn diagram (see Figure 4.1, p. 53). The diagram graphically depicts the interdependence of the work that must take place within schools. Because that interdependence strengthens a school while also making it more complex, a high degree of educational leadership is required in all areas and at all levels of leadership. Set aside operations management for the moment and instead focus on the three skills that NASSP has identified for effective educational leadership: setting instructional direction, teamwork, and sensitivity. What happens when those skills aren't in evidence? It's every teacher and administrator for him- or herself! No unifying vision or direction or collaboration exists at any level and decisions are made at the top with little or no input and respect for the professional experience of other leaders throughout the school. With a focus on collaborative leadership and improved student performance, a lack of direction, teamwork, or sensitivity results in chaos. So how does a school leader become more proficient in these three skills?

Each of the next three sections will discuss one of the skills as well as the behavioral indicators that can be analyzed and practiced. It is necessary to break each of the skills into discrete components (behavioral indicators and descriptors of practice) to better enable you to analyze your own performance. Further, each skill is divided into four subsections to help you to understand the concepts more fully and to conduct your self-analysis methodically:

- A definition of the term
- Behavioral indicators and descriptors of practice
- Personal development tools and activities that can help you practice the skill to build capacity and effectiveness
- Examples of other school leaders putting the behaviors in action.

## Skill: Setting Instructional Direction

**Defined:** Implementing strategies for improving teaching and learning, including putting programs and improvement efforts into action. Developing a vision of learning and establishing clear goals; providing direction in achieving stated goals; encouraging others to contribute to goal achievement; securing commitment to a course of action from individuals and groups.

Behavioral indicators for setting instructional direction:

- Articulates a vision related to teaching and learning
- Articulates high performance expectations for self or others
- Encourages improvement in teaching and learning
- Sets clear measurable objectives
- Generates enthusiasm toward common goals
- Seeks to develop alliances outside the school to support high quality teaching and learning
- Acknowledges achievement or accomplishments
- Seeks commitment to a course of action.

## How Do *You* Put It in Action?

### Activity #1

To begin to self-assess your capacity in **setting instructional direction**, reflect on what it looks like when you perform each of the behaviors. List some specific examples from your own practice as evidence that you can and do perform each behavior.

| Personal Reflection: My View | |
| --- | --- |
| **Behavior/descriptor** | **Give examples of your performance of this behavior and the frequency with which it occurs. Be specific.** |
| Articulates a vision related to teaching and learning | |
| Articulates high performance expectations for self or others | |
| Encourages improvement in teaching and learning | |
| Sets clear measurable objectives | |
| Generates enthusiasm toward common goals | |
| Seeks to develop alliances outside the school to support high-quality teaching and learning | |
| Acknowledges achievement or accomplishments | |
| Seeks commitment to a course of action | |

## Activity #2

Discuss **setting instructional direction** and its indicators with your supervisor, mentor, or coach. Elicit feedback regarding your effectiveness in demonstrating these skills. Discuss strategies for practice that builds greater capacity.

| Feedback: View of a Colleague, Supervisor, Mentor, or Coach | | |
| --- | --- | --- |
| **Behavior/descriptor** | **Effectiveness in demonstrating** | **Strategies to build capacity** |
| Articulates a vision related to teaching and learning | | |
| Articulates high performance expectations for self or others | | |
| Encourages improvement in teaching and learning | | |
| Sets clear measurable objectives | | |
| Generates enthusiasm toward common goals | | |
| Seeks to develop alliances outside the school to support high-quality teaching and learning | | |
| Acknowledges achievement or accomplishments | | |
| Seeks commitment to a course of action | | |

**Activity #3**

Complete the following chart to assess your ability in this skill. You will use the results to develop your personal learning plan in Chapter 7.

| Setting Instructional Direction: How Do *You* Put It in Action? | |
| --- | --- |
| **Gather & Analyze Data** | **Ask:** How is my on-the-job performance in this skill area?<br><br>■ Reflect on your performance of the setting instructional direction behavioral indicators—the frequency of engagement in each behavior as opposed to the ability to perform the behavior.<br><br>■ Solicit face-to-face feedback from a variety of sources—such as a mentor, a coach, a supervisor, supervisees, and colleagues—that focuses on the setting instructional direction indicators.<br><br>■ Seek anonymous feedback from the 360-degree tool available from NASSP (www.principals.org).<br><br>■ Seek data from a formal assessment process (e.g., Selecting and Developing 21st Century Leaders and Leadership Skills Assessments from NASSP).<br><br>■ Review your performance on the indicators. Discuss the results with a mentor or a colleague. |
| **Possible Solutions & Strategies** | Assignments that stretch and provide practice in this skill:<br><br>_____<br><br>_____<br><br>_____<br><br>■ Accept leadership of an ad hoc group with a difficult task, a group of inexperienced or unskilled people, or a loosely structured group to practice bringing structure and direction to a group in order to accomplish tasks.<br><br>■ Convene a committee or task force to study an issue regarding teaching and learning. Use a written charge that you have drafted for that group. In that charge, include the specific purpose and objectives for the group related to improved learning, the advisory or decision-making status of the group, resources that are available to assist in the group's work, to whom the group will report, your expectations, and deadlines or a timeline.<br><br>■ Meet regularly with staff to discuss their priorities. Provide input on the basis of your expectations as instructional leader in the organization.<br><br>■ Study group dynamics in actual work groups and identify the behaviors that assist or hinder the groups in completing their tasks.<br><br>■ Seek opportunities to chair problem-solving committees at the school or district level. Ask a mentor or colleague to monitor your progress and provide feedback regarding the effective use of planning skills and follow-through.<br><br>■ Organize your administrative team into focus groups. Create a cadre to train aspiring leaders within your own school or district and lead this group yourself. |

| **Possible Solutions & Strategies** | **Workshops, seminars, and courses** |
|---|---|
| | _____ |
| | _____ |
| | _____ |
| | ■ Attend training on new instructional methods and procedures to find new and better ways of doing things in the classroom and include faculty members. Check your district, regional service agency, state department, or colleges and universities in your area for opportunities for building capacity in this skill area. |
| | **Mentor, coaches, supervisors** |
| | **Ask:** Who can mentor me in this area and help me prioritize issues? |
| | _____ |
| | _____ |
| | _____ |
| | What are the questions I can ask a mentor about behavior and practice in this area? |
| | _____ |
| | _____ |
| | _____ |
| | ■ Discuss actual school issues with a mentor, focusing on the effective school leader's use of skills in judgment and results orientation to set high priorities for instructional leadership and the management of learning. |
| | **Readings** (see Appendix 5 for an extensive list) |
| | Bennis, W. (2009). *On becoming a leader: The leadership classic.* Revised and Updated. Philadelphia, PA: Basic Books. |
| | Blanchard, K., Carew, D., and Parisi-Carew, E. (2009). *The one minute manager builds high performing teams: Excellence through team building.* New York, NY: William Morrow. |
| | Blasé, J. J. and Kirby, P. C. *Bringing out the best in teachers: What effective principals do.* Second Edition. Thousand Oaks, CA: Corwin Press, 2000. |
| | Carnegie, D. & Associates. (2001). *The leader in you: How to win friends, influence people, and succeed in a changing world.* New York, NY: Simon & Schuster. |
| | **Off-the-job development opportunities** |
| | **Ask:** What organizations and committees can I become active in to practice the behaviors? |
| | _____ |
| | _____ |
| | _____ |
| | **NASSP professional development opportunities** |
| | ■ Online courses |
| | ■ Seminars |
| | ■ Web-based resources |
| | ■ Customized professional development |
| | (Visit www.principals.org/ProfessionalDevelopment.aspx to see current offerings.) |

| | |
|---|---|
| **Assess Readiness & Build Capacity** | **Ask:** Who will be affected by my personal development activities in this skill area? How?<br><br>_____<br>_____<br>_____<br><br>What specific development in this skill area can I engage to have the greatest impact on my personal/professional capacity and the needs of the school?<br><br>_____<br>_____<br>_____<br><br>What school data (e.g., achievement; attendance, graduation, and dropout rates; demographics; and instructional staff qualifications, experience, and background) affect my professional development needs and the possible solutions I identified above? How?<br><br>_____<br>_____<br>_____ |
| **Create & Communicate Plan** | See page 109 to develop your plan.<br>**Ask:** How will I share my personal learning plan with others?<br><br>_____<br>_____<br>_____<br><br>Specifically, how will I encourage every adult in my school to create a learning plan that is based on their developmental needs in the context of the needs of the school and the students?<br><br>_____<br>_____<br>_____ |
| **Implement Plan** | This is how I will practice the indicators to build capacity in the skill:<br><br>_____<br>_____<br>_____ |

| **Monitor & Adjust** | These are the specific measures of progress I will use in this skill area:<br><br>_____<br>_____<br>_____<br><br>These are the specific measures of progress I will use to determine the impact my progress in this area is having on the needs of the school:<br><br>_____<br>_____<br>_____<br><br>This is the feedback I will solicit: (when, from whom, in what form):<br><br>_____<br>_____<br>_____<br><br>I will use these aids to help in my development (e.g., reflection, journaling):<br><br>_____<br>_____<br>_____<br><br>Return to "Gather & Analyze Data" at the beginning of this instrument to establish new priorities with the same skill or to begin work on another skill. |
|---|---|

## How Your Colleagues Put It in Action

Below you will find excerpts from interviews with several middle level and high school leaders related to their efforts to **set instructional direction**.

"Being a high school principal is hard. To be a leader is to be a servant leader, to be out there doing good for other people....The volume of things that one is expected to be good at is huge. It's bigger than it's ever been. Those things always have to be done. [In addition] all of the teachers expect me to be knowledgeable. I don't have to be an expert in everything they teach, but I need to be knowledgeable in the content, in the pedagogy, in being able to be an advocate for them.... [When we know] what it takes for students to be successful and can be a partner with them, then that makes a lot of the difference. At this school learning is first.

"What's important here is that this isn't Mark Wilson's vision for the school, this is a vision that has been in part built by our community, by our students, by our school board, by our teachers. If I were to leave, we have a system in place...this work can continue. And that's exciting ...because it's important to find things that you can do in schools that are successful, and things that have sustainability. The expectations of what we've done here, the structures that we've put in place, the vision and philosophy and

*10 Skills for Successful School Leaders*

beliefs we have reached together and stated as our own, those are things that belong to a lot of people."

— Mark Wilson, Principal, Morgan County High School, Madison, GA,
MetLife/NASSP 2009 National High School Principal of the Year

"I need to be the one that's up on all the new techniques and the different strategies, I can't stress that enough. It's those principals that are the instructional leaders that see the most success in their schools. Once you determine what the best practices are, you need to practice what you preach. If you say that classroom time is important, then from the principal's office, you need to preserve that good quality classroom time, and you don't need to interrupt classes with the intercom and things. You have to protect that valuable time.

"And also, you have to let the teachers know that they can make a difference in the lives of boys and girls, and that they have the power to do that. It doesn't matter how that child comes into the classroom. It doesn't matter where that child comes from. It doesn't matter where that child lives. It doesn't matter who their mom and dad are, or who they're living with, or what their standard of living is. We have to feel in our hearts that we can make a difference in the lives of those boys and girls, each and every day. And from that, we develop a new culture and we feel that we can make a difference in the lives of boys and girls. And that empowers our teachers to be the very best that they can be. And from that you build capacity…. You need to be persistent. You need to make sure that you don't forget, each and every day, what your purpose is in the school. And sometimes that's difficult.

"At Boaz Middle School we look at every day, every child, a success. We want our children to enjoy some sort of success, each and every day. And we build upon those successes. And we need to focus on baby steps. We need to celebrate everything. In the beginning, eight years ago when we first started implementing our professional learning community, we had small successes, and we just built on those successes and we made sure that we emphasized the positive things and grew from that."

—Ray Landers, Principal, Boaz (AL) Middle School,
MetLife/NASSP 2009 National Middle Level Principal of the Year

"When I became principal it was the second year of our school…in the first year they had three different principals. And because of that, there was a lot of confusion between students and staff about the direction that the school was going. I knew that it was essential that teachers and staff have a solid horizon or a vision to focus on…clear, attainable and realistic—something we could do. So we started out with baby steps at first, because many staff members had to build that trust with me, as the new principal. We started with little successes, and then we increased our success each and every year. Don't expect any kind of change to happen overnight. And don't just change for the sake of changing. You have to really look at your school and your school community and decide that change is necessary and [understand] that everyone may not be open to that change, even if they know it's needed.

"Making sure that teachers have a voice in what goes on at our school every day is essential…if you come to visit any day, from the custodian to me, every person has a voice here. We established a leadership council, which is made up of department chairs, first-year teachers, paraprofessionals, and classifieds…the leadership council helps lead the way for us and empowers the staff members in the decision-making process.

"Stay true to the vision…the vision has to be a part of the principal. If the principal doesn't believe in the vision, there's no way that anyone else on the campus is going to. You have to be that vision every single day. A personal motto: I commit to making a positive difference every single day."

—Delic Loyde, Principal, Stelle Claughton Middle School, Houston, TX, a 2009 MetLife-NASSP Breakthrough School

---

"One official once told me after sitting through an entire administrative meeting [at my school] that "everything discussed was related to instruction—teaching and learning." School leaders must have one and only one focus—teaching and learning. Everything we do affects the classroom.

"Over time, the staff moved from the role of observer to participant to leader and finally to co-owner. Sustainability is about distributed leadership throughout the school, shared responsibility, and shared ownership. In high-performing schools, the staff owns the decisions, the plans, the outcomes, and most importantly, they own all of the students."

—Mel Riddile, NASSP

---

"Our scores were at 92%, but we realized that we were failing our students of color and literacy was a challenge. We decided to take a small team to a conference so they could pilot our literacy initiative. But when they returned, the other 7th-grade team wanted to become involved, and the following year, we felt that we were positioned to bring a literacy tactic into our school improvement plan—so the literacy initiative became schoolwide. Our mantra became "mile deep rather than mile wide," focusing our vision and all professional development in one area rather than letting us get distracted. The focus was on collaborative leadership…not about me but about dedicated leaders who saw that students were not reading text in the manner they should.

"Teachers became invested and wanted students to achieve and think at a higher level; team leaders and department chairs became leaders. When I said I wasn't satisfied that we were failing a group of students, one of my chairs said that we should be increasing literacy for all students…a culture of literacy needs to permeate the building. Collaborative leadership is not only my style but is where we have had success…a building leader is only as good as those he or she surrounds himself or herself with…leaders at all levels need to be persistent and passionate."

—Terry Wolfson, Principal, Hopkins West Jr. High School, Minnetonka, MN

**Activity #4**

To practice identifying behavioral indicators that are related to **setting instructional direction**, list the indicators that you recognize in the actions of those school leaders.

| Behavioral Indicators Identified | Practice, Action, or Sentiment From Interviews |
|---|---|
|  |  |
|  |  |
|  |  |
|  |  |

## Skill: Teamwork

**Defined:** Seeking and encouraging involvement of team members. Modeling and encouraging the behaviors that move the group to the completion of a task. Supporting group accomplishment.

Behavioral indicators of teamwork:

- Supports the ideas of team members
- Encourages team members to share ideas
- Contributes ideas toward accomplishing the team's goals
- Assists in performing the operational tasks of the team
- Seeks input from team members
- Acts to maintain direction or focus to achieve the team's goals
- Seeks consensus among team members.

## How Do *You* Put It in Action?

### Activity #1

To begin to self-assess your capacity in **teamwork**, reflect on what it looks like when you perform each of the behaviors. List some specific examples from your own practice as evidence that you can and do perform this behavior.

| Personal Reflection: My View | |
| --- | --- |
| **Behavior/descriptor** | **Give examples of your performance of this behavior and the frequency with which it occurs. Be specific.** |
| Supports the ideas of team members | |
| Encourages team members to share ideas | |
| Contributes ideas toward accomplishing the team's goals | |
| Assists in performing the operational tasks of the team | |
| Seeks input from team members | |
| Acts to maintain direction or focus to achieve the team's goals | |
| Seeks consensus among team members | |

## Activity #2

Discuss **teamwork** and its indicators with your supervisor, mentor, or coach. Elicit feedback regarding your effectiveness in demonstrating these skills. Discuss strategies for practice that builds greater capacity.

| Feedback: View of a Colleague, Supervisor, Mentor, or Coach | | |
| --- | --- | --- |
| **Behavior/descriptor** | **Effectiveness in demonstrating** | **Strategies to build capacity** |
| Supports the ideas of team members | | |
| Encourages team members to share ideas | | |
| Contributes ideas toward accomplishing the team's goals | | |
| Assists in performing the operational tasks of the team | | |
| Seeks input from team members | | |
| Acts to maintain direction or focus to achieve the team's goals | | |
| Seeks consensus among team members | | |

## Activity #3

Complete the following chart to assess your ability in this skill. You will use the results to develop your personal learning plan in Chapter 7.

| Teamwork: How Do *You* Put It in Action? | |
|---|---|
| **Gather & Analyze Data** | **Ask:** How is my on-the-job performance in this skill area?<br><br>■ Reflect on your performance of the teamwork behavioral indicators—the frequency of engagement in each behavior as opposed to the ability to perform the behavior.<br><br>■ Solicit face-to-face feedback from a variety of sources—such as a mentor, a coach, a supervisor, supervisees, and colleagues—that focuses on the teamwork indicators.<br><br>■ Seek anonymous feedback from the 360-degree tool available from NASSP (www.principals.org).<br><br>■ Seek data from a formal assessment process (e.g., Selecting and Developing 21st Century Leaders and Leadership Skills Assessments from NASSP).<br><br>■ Review your performance on the indicators. Discuss the results with a mentor or a colleague. |
| **Possible Solutions & Strategies** | Assignments that stretch and provide practice in this skill:<br><br>_____<br><br>_____<br><br>_____<br><br>■ Conduct an assessment of the culture in your school or district to determine the atmosphere for risk taking, meeting needs, and so on. With your team, develop a plan to improve the culture as needed. Understand that culture is nurtured, not discovered.<br><br>■ Develop strategies to challenge employees to bring a possible solution with every problem.<br><br>■ Monitor the work of groups of staff members. Maintain records of the involvement of staff members in activities and events such as committees, work groups, and task forces. As you develop new groups or committees, rotate or add new individuals to groups to foster their development<br><br>■ Practice seeking input and advice from others. Incorporate appropriate advice into planning and decision making. Give appropriate credit to others for suggestions, advice, and assistance.<br><br>■ Establish a group of people who are known as the key communicators within the school from whom you can solicit ideas, questions, and reactions to proposals. Make sure all stakeholder groups are represented, including teachers, other administrators, classified personnel, retired persons, business partners, students, and parents. Use this group to continually assess the needs of the diverse constituencies in your school community. |

| **Possible Solutions & Strategies** | ■ Practice working with people to help others get the job done. Engage in self-directed learning such as maintaining a daily journal in which you note conversations and other interactions. At the end of each day, review your notes and reflect on how your words and actions were perceived by others. Such an analysis may indicate the need or desire for other development activities. |
|---|---|

■ Evaluate your organizational structure by focusing on providing maximum opportunity for each staff member to contribute to the success of the school.

■ Organize your administrative team into focus groups. Create a cadre to train aspiring leaders within your own school or district and lead this group yourself.

**Workshops, seminars, and courses**

_____

_____

_____

Check your district, regional service agency, state department, and local colleges and universities for opportunities to build capacity in this skill area.

**Mentor, coaches, supervisors**

**Ask:** Who can mentor me in this area and help me prioritize issues?

_____

_____

_____

What are the questions I can ask a mentor about behavior and practice in this area?

_____

_____

_____

**Readings** (see Appendix 5 for an extensive list)

Bennis, W. & Nanus, B. (2003). *Leaders: The strategies for taking charge.* New York, NY: HarperBusiness Essentials.

Blanchard, K. & Bowles, S. (1997). *Gung ho: Turn on the people in any organization.* New York, NY: William Morrow.

Blankstein, A. M., Houston, P. D., & Cole, R. W. (2008). *Sustaining professional learning communities.* Thousand Oaks, CA: Corwin.

**Off-the-job development opportunities**

Ask: What organizations and committees can I become active in to practice the behaviors?

_____

_____

_____

**NASSP professional development opportunities**

■ Online courses

■ Seminars

■ Web-based resources

■ Customized professional development

(Visit www.principals.org/ProfessionalDevelopment.aspx to see current offerings.)

| | |
|---|---|
| **Assess Readiness & Build Capacity** | **Ask:** Who will be affected by my personal development activities in this skill area? How? <br><br>_____<br>_____<br>_____<br><br>What specific development in this skill area can I engage in that will have the greatest impact on personal/professional capacity and the needs of the school?<br><br>_____<br>_____<br>_____<br><br>What school data (e.g., achievement; attendance, graduation, and drop-out rates; demographics; and instructional staff qualifications, experience, and background) affect my professional development needs and the possible solutions I identified above? How?<br><br>_____<br>_____<br>_____ |
| **Create & Communicate Plan** | See page 109 to develop your plan.<br>**Ask:** How will I share my personal learning plan with others?<br><br>_____<br>_____<br>_____<br><br>Specifically, how will I encourage every adult in my school to have a learning plan based on their developmental needs in the context of the needs of the school and the students?<br><br>_____<br>_____<br>_____ |
| **Implement Plan** | This is how I will practice the indicators to build capacity in the skill:<br><br>_____<br>_____<br>_____ |

| **Monitor & Adjust** | These are the specific measures of progress I will use in this skill area:<br>_____<br>_____<br>_____<br><br>These are the specific measures of progress I will use to determine the impact my progress in this area is having on the needs of the school:<br>_____<br>_____<br>_____<br><br>This is the feedback I will solicit: (when, from whom, in what form):<br>_____<br>_____<br>_____<br><br>I will use these aids to help in my development (e.g., reflection, journaling):<br>_____<br>_____<br>_____<br><br>Return to "Gather and Analyze Data" at the beginning of this instrument to establish new priorities within the same skill or to begin work on another skill. |
| --- | --- |

## How Your Colleagues Put It in Action

Below you will find excerpts from interviews of several middle level and high school leaders that are related to **teamwork**.

"Well, of course, the principal ultimately is the leader. There are thousands and thousands of decisions to be made each day. But to develop the framework in which those decisions are made…to have the opportunity to really move forward, you've got to have people who are connected and [empowered to] make decisions. In our school, we have a leadership council. And it's through that collaboration that we have done most of our best work. [We ask] "OK, now what do we want each of these groups listed (teachers, administrators, principals, students) to do that they're not doing now? And what do we want them to continue doing that they're doing well?" Many of our major initiatives have sprung from that.

"In terms of hiring, I put together a committee of teachers and we all review the applications and decide who we're going to invite in for an interview. I don't sit in on the initial interviews (teachers who will work with this person do). Once a candidate has gone through that process, we bring them to the school and they spend an entire day in the classes of the teachers that they would be working with. It gives us a real opportunity to be able to see whether that person fits with us, and the candidate can see whether we're what they're looking for. In doing that, once we've brought somebody on board, there are half a dozen people who are invested in that person's success.

"Our teachers are committed to each other because the work they're doing is so interwoven. There are endless possibilities for our teachers to collaborate and work together and not just [to] 'make their job easier,' because that's not what it's about. It's to make their work more productive. And, if their work is more productive, then they're more effective as teachers.

"We've celebrated our success. People are motivated by their hearts and their heads. And when you motivate their heads you've got to give them data. They have to be able to look at this and say, "You know, well gosh, this does work." But people are also motivated by their hearts, and you make a lot of difference when you're out [in the halls and at activities]. If you're in your office and not with the people, you're missing an opportunity."

—Mark Wilson, Principal, Morgan County High School, Madison, GA,
MetLife/NASSP 2009 National High School Principal of the Year

---

"I can't do everything by myself, and I know over the last few years we've heard a lot about collaborative decision making and shared responsibility—but when I started in the business over 30 years ago, that wasn't at the forefront—the principal was considered to be the head of the school and everything flowed through [him or her]. That's not what it's all about today—it's about sharing that responsibility and empowering those teachers so that collaborative decision making can take place in your building. We all have great ideas. There's room at the table for a lot of different ideas, a lot of different styles, a lot of different teaching methods.... Collaborative decision making can never be underestimated. To have a group of teachers that have been empowered to make collaborative decisions, that's one of the best things that you could do in school."

—Ray Landers, Principal, Boaz (AL) Middle School,
MetLife/NASSP 2009 National Middle Level Principal of the Year

---

"We have worked hard over the last three years to develop a culture where everyone has value and everyone is important and to develop and communicate a shared vision: excellence for each and every student, excellence in every endeavor. Be approachable and visible, accessible to staff, students and parents. I began by having open-agenda meetings with each staff member…basically I dedicated time to talk one-on-one with each and every staff member. And then I opened it up to parents on a couple of nights, and also to students, to really hear what was on their hearts about their school—what they felt about where the school was at the present time, and what they wanted the school to become. And by looking at all of that information, after those meetings, we developed that vision. We could see where our school could go and what our school could become. We developed a sense of team. We [also] have student teams that have a voice in our school, we ask our students what they like, what they see working, what is not working. We have the leadership council, we have the department chairs, grade-level team leaders, we have academic families or academic teams, and they all intermingle or interlock with each other in meetings. We have a regular system of time that we allot and commit as a priority to share information and to share ideas so we all work together for student success."

—Delic Loyde, Principal, Stelle Claughton Middle School, Houston, TX,
2009 MetLife-NASSP Breakthrough School

"I suppose it has to start with a leader who believes in collaborative leadership and isn't threatened by it. That mind-set is found in leaders who are risk takers and encourage those around them to take risks to improve the quality of education their students receive. Another key component is that teachers know they must want to be a part of this process. Too often, teachers talk about wanting the opportunities that come with leadership but often they only want the opportunities and not the responsibilities."

—Theresa Hinkle, retired teacher, Greensboro, NC

"Collaborative leadership was a priority from day one. Year one, the only "change" I made was to establish a school leadership team. This group was comprised of the entire administrative team (principal, APs, deans), all subject-area lead teachers, the librarian, the reading specialist, the lead counselor, and the technology resource teacher. This was a significant shift for some "leaders" who were in fact paper pushers. Some of these folks bowed out gracefully at the end of year one as I made it clear that shared leadership was of utmost importance and key to our advancement. Now, three full years later, we have a team of true leaders assembled. We meet two times monthly. All major school decisions are made by this group. This group also acts as our school improvement team (SIP) and monitors the plan that is constructed by all staff. The team has also evolved to include the cafeteria manager. Parents meet with us quarterly to review our progress on the SIP and offer guidance from a parent perspective. This group consults with our student government officers when necessary. Collaborative leadership is also supported via our team leader structure to our interdisciplinary teams. This leader changes quarterly, and they, too, are invited to attend school leadership team meetings."

—Janice Koslowsky, Principal, Potomac Falls High School, Sterling, VA

## Activity #4

To practice identifying behavioral indicators related to **teamwork**, list the indicators that you saw in the actions of these school leaders.

| Behavioral Indicators Identified | Practice, Action, or Sentiment From Interviews |
|---|---|
|  |  |
|  |  |
|  |  |

## Skill: Sensitivity

**Defined:** Perceiving the needs and concerns of others; dealing tactfully with others in emotionally stressful situations or in conflict. Knowing what information to communicate and to whom. Relating to people of varying ethnic, cultural, and religious backgrounds.

Behavioral indicators for sensitivity:
- Interacts professionally and tactfully with others
- Elicits perceptions, feelings, or concerns of others
- Voices disagreement without creating unnecessary conflict
- Communicates necessary information to appropriate persons in a timely manner
- Expresses written, verbal, and/or nonverbal recognition of feelings, needs, or concerns in responding to others.

## How Do *You* Put the Skill in Action?

### Activity #1

To begin to self assess your capacity in **sensitivity**, reflect on what it looks like when you perform each of the behaviors. List some specific examples from your own practice that could serve as evidence that you can and do perform this behavior.

| Personal Reflection: My View | |
| --- | --- |
| **Behavior/descriptor** | **Give examples of your performance of this behavior and the frequency with which it occurs. Be specific.** |
| Interacts professionally and tactfully with others | |
| Elicits perceptions, feelings, or concerns of others | |
| Voices disagreement without creating unnecessary conflict | |
| Communicates necessary information to appropriate persons in a timely manner | |
| Expresses written, verbal, and nonverbal recognition of feelings, needs, or concerns in responding to others | |

**Activity #2**

Discuss **sensitivity** and its indicators with your supervisor, mentor, or coach. Elicit feedback regarding your effectiveness in demonstrating these skills. Discuss strategies for practicing to build greater capacity.

| Feedback: View of a Colleague, Supervisor, Mentor, or Coach | | |
| --- | --- | --- |
| **Behavior/descriptor** | **Effectiveness in demonstrating** | **Strategies to build capacity** |
| Interacts professionally and tactfully with others | | |
| Elicits perceptions, feelings, or concerns of others | | |
| Voices disagreement without creating unnecessary conflict | | |
| Communicates necessary information to appropriate persons in a timely manner | | |
| Expresses written, verbal, and/or nonverbal recognition of feelings, needs, or concerns in responding to others | | |

## Activity #3

Complete the following chart to assess your ability in this skill. You will use the results to develop your personal learning plan in Chapter 7.

| Sensitivity: How Do *You* Put It in Action? | |
|---|---|
| **Gather & Analyze Data** | **Ask:** How is my on-the-job performance in this skill area?<br><br>■ Reflect on your performance of the sensitivity behavioral indicators—the frequency with which you engage in each behavior as opposed to the ability to perform the behavior.<br><br>■ Solicit face-to-face feedback from a variety of sources—such as a mentor, a coach, a supervisor, supervisees, and colleagues—that focuses on the sensitivity indicators.<br><br>■ Seek anonymous feedback from the 360-degree tool available from NASSP (www.principals.org).<br><br>■ Seek data from a formal assessment process (e.g., Selecting and Developing 21st Century Leaders and Leadership Skills Assessments from NASSP).<br><br>■ Review your performance on the indicators. Discuss the results with a mentor or a colleague. |
| **Possible Solutions & Strategies** | Assignments that stretch and provide practice in this skill:<br><br>_____<br><br>_____<br><br>_____<br><br><br>■ Determine who in each area should receive what type of information. Regularly and systematically provide appropriate information to those people.<br><br>■ Develop individual and school communication plans similar to your district's communication plan. Ensure that all affected staff members have copies of the necessary documents, letters, and other information.<br><br>■ Practice active listening in group settings. Make statements that indicate that you have heard correctly, understand, and respect the comments of others.<br><br>■ Practice responding directly (in person, by phone, or in writing) to people who express needs, problems, or concerns. .<br><br>■ Practice delegating tasks to others in the group to increase their sense of belonging and accomplishment when the task is completed.<br><br>■ To practice collecting behavioral data and giving feedback in a sensitive manner, serve as a peer coach to a colleague. |

| | |
|---|---|
| **Possible Solutions & Strategies** | **Workshops, seminars, and courses**<br><br>_____<br>_____<br>_____ |

- Check your district, regional service agency, state department, or colleges and universities in your area for opportunities for building capacity in this skill area.

**Mentor, coaches, supervisors**

**Ask:** Who can mentor me in this area and help me prioritize issues?

_____
_____
_____

- What are the questions I can ask a mentor about behavior and practice in this area?

**Readings** (see Appendix 5 for an extensive list)

Brounstein, M. (1993). _Handling the difficult employee: Solving performance problems_. Menlo Park, CA: Crisp Publications.

Colvin, G. (2007). _Seven steps for developing a proactive schoolwide discipline plan: A guide for principals and leadership teams_. Thousand Oaks, CA: Corwin.

Crowe, S. A. (1998). _Since strangling isn't an option... Dealing with difficult people—common problems and uncommon solutions_. New York, NY: Perigee.

**Off-the-job development opportunities**

**Ask:** What organizations and committees can I become active in to practice the behaviors?

_____
_____
_____

To become more aware of the needs, concerns, and problems of people from different backgrounds, volunteer to work in a community organization that serves the needs of people.

**NASSP professional development opportunities**

- Online courses
- Seminars
- Web-based resources
- Customized professional development

(Visit www.principals.org/ProfessionalDevelopment.aspx to see current offerings.)

## Sensitivity: How Do *You* Put It in Action?

| | |
|---|---|
| **Assess Readiness & Build Capacity** | **Ask:** What do climate surveys, such as CASE from NASSP, tell me about the readiness and capacity of the school community (faculty members, students, and parents) that will affect whether and how I will implement a solution? <br><br>_____ <br>_____ <br>_____ <br><br>Who will be affected by my personal development activities in this skill area? How? <br><br>_____ <br>_____ <br>_____ <br><br>What specific development in this skill area can I engage in that will have the greatest impact on my personal and professional capacity and the needs of the school? <br><br>_____ <br>_____ <br>_____ <br><br>What school data (e.g., achievement; attendance, graduation, and drop-out rates; demographics; and instructional staff qualifications, experience, and background) affects my professional development needs and the possible solutions I identified above? How? <br><br>_____ <br>_____ <br>_____ |
| **Create & Communicate Plan** | See page 109 to develop your plan. <br>**Ask:** How will I share my personal learning plan with others? <br><br>_____ <br>_____ <br>_____ <br><br>Specifically how will I encourage every adult in my school to have a learning plan based on their developmental needs in the context of the needs of the school and the students? <br><br>_____ <br>_____ <br>_____ |
| **Implement Plan** | This is how I will practice the indicators to build capacity in the skill: <br><br>_____ <br>_____ <br>_____ |

| **Monitor & Adjust** | These are the specific measures of progress I will use in this skill area: |
| --- | --- |
| | _____<br>_____<br>_____ |
| | These are the specific measures of progress I will use to determine the impact my progress in this area is having on the needs of the school: |
| | _____<br>_____<br>_____ |
| | This is the feedback I will solicit: (when, from whom, in what form): |
| | _____<br>_____<br>_____ |
| | I will use these aids to help in my development (e.g., reflection, journaling): |
| | _____<br>_____<br>_____ |
| | Return to "Gather & Analyze Data" at the beginning of this instrument to establish new priorities within the same skill or to begin work on another skill. |

## How Your Colleagues Put It in Action

Below you will find excerpts from interviews with several middle level and high school leaders related to **sensitivity**.

"Communication breakdown often happens when stress, emotions, and frustrations are running high, and at times like this, the principal has the difficult responsibility of getting everyone riding down the conflict escalator rather than up. My school was once faced with a serious situation and the staff became divided on the issue—sides were taken and lines were being drawn. An already difficult situation was exacerbated when the media ran the story, parents were drawn into the issue, and lawyers got involved—communication with all parties was strained to say the least. Recognizing that time spent in the bathroom taking deep breaths and reminding myself that I could get through this was not helping resolve the problem, I decided it was time to confront the issue head-on with the staff. Because of the high emotional toll the situation had taken on everyone, I wanted to be very sure that I communicated clearly and said what I felt needed to be said. Even though it wasn't my normal style, I wrote a letter to the staff and read it during a staff meeting—this made sure I didn't get sidetracked or forget how I wanted to say something. I could use eye contact, body language, and tone of voice to help convey the message, and afterwards I could give out copies to those who were absent (or anyone else who wanted to reread it, and many did). In short, the message assured everyone they had a right to their own opinion on the issue and that we would get through it, but what we needed to begin asking ourselves was what we wanted to look like once we were on the other side. We were on the brink of destroying the culture we had created and needed to decide if that was what we really wanted to do. I can't say that things changed overnight, but it was the turning point for how we interacted with one another as we continued to work through the situation. And we did come out on the other side with a better appreciation of the role that open communication plays in maintaining a healthy school culture."

—Patti Kinney, NASSP, excerpted from *Voices of Experience:*
*Perspectives from Successful Middle Level Leaders* (2010), National Middle School Association

---

"One of the most important aspects of sensitivity was not only understanding the needs and concerns of others, but also actually doing something about them. As our change efforts grew and matured, I spent more and more time removing barriers and influencing up through the district and through the school on behalf of the needs of the staff. Teachers can't teach if there is chaos in the hallways. Teachers can't offer after-school programs if no one shows up. They viewed me as sensitive to their needs when I actually took action to do something about their issues. Rogerian reflection and feedback is certainly a part of being sensitive, but the real sensitivity is demonstrated through the will to act even when it is not convenient or popular. A sensitive parent may listen to, empathize with and love their child, but when the child tries to run into the street, they must take action. They must love them enough to stop them even if the child doesn't like it. School leaders have to love their staff enough to be willing to risk being disliked by their superiors in order to get their staff members what they need."

—Mel Riddile, NASSP

---

"It is important to make sure that you make yourself available for everyone to be able to discuss their issues and ideas with you. Be a listener. Sometimes people just want to heard and valued. Everyone is not always expecting you to solve the problem. Always ask the person what they believe the solution to the issue is. It may be the solution that you have been looking for."

—Maria Bradley, Principal, Gladden Middle School, Chatsworth, GA

---

"I continually remind myself that I serve many constituencies (students, families, staff, and the district), always keeping in mind that student best interest should never be compromised. I tell staff that while I will support them in any way that I can, that support unfortunately cannot always be unconditional. I believe it is important to practice and model respectful direct communication. For example, when a parent calls to complain or question the practice of a teacher, I will ask whether or not the parent has contacted the teacher. If not, I will encourage the parent to connect with the teacher first, always letting them know that I want to know how the conversation went—positively or negatively. For the most part, I find that it was a mere miscommunication and most often easily resolved."

—Terry Wolfson, Principal, Hopkins West Jr. High School, Minnetonka, MN

"We remain sensitive to recognizing all employees and valuing their individual role and contribution to the smooth and transparent functioning of a school day. We take the time to meet with the supporting service staff to outline our school year goals, themes and school improvement goals. We also share student AYP data and explain our initiatives to the greater community."

—Stacey Kopnitsky, Assistant Principal, Cabin John Middle School,
Montgomery County Public Schools, Potomac, MD

## Activity #4

To practice identifying behavioral indicators related to **sensitivity**, list the indicators that you saw in the actions of these school leaders.

| Behavioral Indicators Identified | Practice, Action, or Sentiment From Interviews |
|---|---|
| | |
| | |
| | |
| | |

# 4 Resolving Complex Problems

*Without craftsmanship, inspiration is a mere reed shaken in the wind.*

—*Johannes Brahms*

## Judgment ■ Results Orientation ■ Organizational Ability

Peruse the dictionary for the word *complex* and you arrive at synonyms for schools: complicated, made up of interrelated parts, interconnected, difficult to analyze and understand, and thorny. Schools are complex places that require formulas not only for success but also for inspiration. School leadership is a craft and an art form. A lay person may wonder why schools are such complex places. After all, it's simply a scaled-up version of one teacher in one classroom teaching algebra or language arts to 20 or 30 students, isn't it?

Of course, it's not so simple. To the leadership team, the principal, the assistant principal, teacher leaders, and everyone within a school the complexities manifest themselves quickly. Set aside the routine challenges associated with getting the students to school, the fire drills, the cafeteria calamities, discipline policies, and so on. For the sake of argument, focus on that one "simple" algebra class where students are not performing up to their potential. The *Breaking Ranks* Venn Diagram (see Figure 4.1) illustrates the interconnectedness and complexities of addressing a simple challenge. Following are just some of the questions that might be asked in this situation to determine how to improve.

- Were the students prepared well enough in previous math classes?
- Do the students have the physical resources that are necessary to help them learn?
- Is the class well-organized and small enough to guarantee personal attention for each student?
- Is the time allotted ample and organized well enough to allow students to learn effectively?
- Is the teacher knowledgeable and well-prepared? Is the teacher effective in conveying the lesson? If not, why not?
- Are the standards rigorous enough? Do they meet the needs of students to qualify for advanced mathematics in later years, including college?
- Are the assessments rigorous and reasonable?
- Do the students care? Is the learning tied to real-world applications?

- Does the teacher care?
- What data points are available and how reliable is the data?
- How can the collection of the appropriate data and proper analysis be ensured?
- Is the teacher working with other teachers on lesson planning?
- Does the teacher understand different learning styles and plan lessons accordingly?
- Does the assessment taking place guide what is taught and how?
- Does each student have a plan to address their deficiencies in this area?

Figure 4.1

**Collaborative Leadership/**
**Professional Learning Communities**
Vision, direction, and focus
Site council
Staff collaboration
Redefine teacher role
Personal learning plans
for principal and teachers
Political/financial alliances
Five-year review

Higher education partnerships
Celebrate diversity
Coaching students

**Curriculum, Instruction,**
**and Assessment**
Essential learnings
Alternatives to tracking
Integrated curriculum
Real-world applications
Knowledgeable teachers
Integrated assessment
K–16 continuity
Integrated technology

**Improved**
**Student**
**Performance**

Small units
Flexible scheduling
Democratic values
90-student maximum

Caring teachers
Activities/service tied
to learning
Community learning
Critical thinking
Learning styles
Youth services

**Personalizing Your School Environment**
Personal plans for progress
Personal adult advocate
Families as partners

Of course, if the school's leaders simply promulgated this list of questions and walked away, they would undoubtedly not be leading for long. If a quick-fix is not appropriate for the situation, the school's leaders may have to engage many different stakeholders in trying to come up with a long-term solution that avoids the pitfalls of impulsive reaction and instead incorporates a feasible and sustainable process:

For too long, educators have looked for a silver bullet that will solve schools' problems. A good idea is read or heard at a conference, brought back to the school, and implemented immediately. In the urgency to solve the problem, changes have been implemented without regard for the big picture. As a consequence, things may look different, but nothing of significance has really changed. School leaders who wish to move beyond this quick-fix mentality must do two things. First, they must recognize the critical role that a school's belief system plays in the sustainability of school improvement efforts. Second, they must carefully examine the process they are employing to implement the change. (NASSP, 2009, pp. 10–11)

Perhaps the algebra classroom fix was relatively easy and entailed providing some additional development for the teacher or new textbooks or finding a new teacher. More often than not, however, the answer is much more complex and requires answering hard questions about yourself—and sometimes requires changing the school's entire belief system. What skills do the principal or assistant principal need to even begin the journey? Such a leader would have to ask—and get answers to—such questions as:

- Have I done what is necessary to identify the cause of the problem?
- Have I analyzed the information appropriately?
- Have I set clear and measurable objectives?
- Have I generated enthusiasm around the goal of improving learning in algebra?
- Have I sought commitment to improvement?
- Have I determined the criteria that indicate a problem is resolved?
- Have I prepared properly for the relevant meetings and do I manage them effectively?

## Behaviors Associated with Resolving Complex Problems

In your role as instructional leader and with your portfolio of operations management tasks, you face truly complex challenges. It is up to you and your team to resolve them with judgment, an orientation towards results, and organizational ability. What happens when those skills aren't in evidence? Leaders make "gut decisions" for the sake of making a decision and without appreciating the implications of a decision. People begin to question their decision-making rationale for even the smallest and seemingly inconsequential things. Staff members are unfocused and do not understand goals or the current course in the journey toward improvement. The leader either feels compelled to do everything or responsibility is delegated yet not effectively monitored, which leads to frustration and mistrust by all involved. Remember, it is relatively easy to make a decision. Making an informed decision is much more difficult.

So how does a school leader become more proficient in judgment, results orientation, and organizational ability? Most leaders—most people—think that their judgment is their strongest suit. In fact, they believe that they have achieved professionally and personally because they have used good judgment. That may very well be the case, but they may still need to practice certain behaviors associated with that skill, such as communicating a clear rationale for their decisions or becoming better at discovering relevant information that should inform decisions.

Each of the next three sections will discuss one of the skills as well as the behavioral indicators that can be analyzed and practiced. It is necessary to break each of the skills into discrete components (behavioral indicators and descriptors of practice) to help you analyze your own performance. Further, each skill is divided into four subsections to help you to understand the concepts more fully and to conduct your analysis methodically:

- A definition of the term
- Behavioral indicators and descriptors of practice
- Personal development tools and activities that can help you practice the skill to build capacity and effectiveness
- Examples of other school leaders putting the behaviors in action.

## Skill: Judgment

**Defined:** Reaching logical conclusions and making high quality decisions on the basis of available information. Giving priority and caution to significant issues. Seeking out relevant data, facts, and impressions. Analyzing and interpreting complex information.

Behavioral indicators of judgment:

- Takes action within the bounds of appropriate priority
- Acts with caution in approaching an unfamiliar person or situation
- Analyzes information to determine the important elements of a situation
- Communicates a clear rationale for a decision
- Seeks additional information
- Uses information sources that are relevant to an issue
- Asks follow-up questions to clarify information
- Seeks to identify the cause of a problem
- Sees relationships among issues.

# How Do *You* Put It in Action?

## Activity #1

To begin to self assess your capacity in **judgment**, reflect on what it looks like when you perform each of the behaviors. List some specific examples from your own practice as evidence that you can and do perform each behavior.

| Personal Reflection: My View | |
| --- | --- |
| **Behavior/descriptor** | **Give examples of your performance of this behavior and the frequency with which it occurs. Be specific.** |
| Takes action within the bounds of appropriate priority | |
| Acts with caution in approaching an unfamiliar person or situation | |
| Analyzes information to determine the important elements of a situation | |
| Communicates a clear rationale for a decision | |
| Seeks additional information | |
| Uses information sources that are relevant to an issue | |
| Asks follow-up questions to clarify information | |
| Seeks to identify the cause of a problem | |
| Sees relationships among issues | |

**Activity #2**

Discuss **judgment** and its indicators with your supervisor, mentor, or coach. Elicit feedback regarding your effectiveness in demonstrating these skills. Discuss strategies for practice that builds greater capacity.

| Feedback: View of a Colleague, Supervisor, Mentor, or Coach | | |
| --- | --- | --- |
| **Behavior/descriptor** | **Effectiveness in demonstrating** | **Strategies to build capacity** |
| Takes action within the bounds of appropriate priority | | |
| Acts with caution in approaching an unfamiliar person or situation | | |
| Analyzes information to determine the important elements of a situation | | |
| Communicates a clear rationale for a decision | | |
| Seeks additional information | | |
| Uses information sources that are relevant to an issue | | |
| Asks follow-up questions to clarify information | | |
| Seeks to identify the cause of a problem | | |
| Sees relationships among issues | | |

**Activity #3**

Complete the following chart to assess your ability in this skill. You will use the results
to develop your personal learning plan in Chapter 7.

| Judgment: How Do *You* Put It in Action? | |
|---|---|
| **Gather & Analyze Data** | **Ask:** How is my on-the-job performance in this skill area?<br><br>■ Reflect on your performance of the judgment behavioral indicators—the frequency with which you engage in each behavior as opposed to your ability to perform the behavior.<br><br>■ Solicit face-to-face feedback from a variety of sources—such as a mentor, a coach, a supervisor, supervisees, and colleagues—that focuses on the judgment indicators.<br><br>■ Seek anonymous feedback from the 360-degree tool available from NASSP (www.principals.org).<br><br>■ Seek data from a formal assessment process (e.g., Selecting and Developing 21st Century Leaders and Leadership Skills Assessments from NASSP).<br><br>■ Review your performance on the indicators. Discuss the results with a mentor or a colleague. |
| **Possible Solutions & Strategies** | Assignments that stretch and provide practice in this skill:<br><br>_____<br>_____<br>_____<br><br><br>■ For a period of time, analyze your information-seeking patterns. List the information pieces considered for each decision, then code each piece as essential, desirable but not essential, or irrelevant. Reflect on your findings to determine whether you are getting the information you need, too little, or too much information to support your decisions.<br><br>■ Practice obtaining information from individuals who present a problem as well as those who are affected by a problem; data in school and district files, and survey instruments; experienced personnel; experts in a problem area; supervisors, mentors, and any other sources specific to the situation.<br><br>■ Before making decisions, practice talking with individuals who will be affected by the decisions to gather additional information and get different perspectives that may lead to more effective decisions.<br><br>■ Seek data from a variety of sources to help you identify problem areas and in determine the causes of problems. Seek assistance from individuals inside and outside the system that can help interpret the data collected.<br><br>■ When presented with a situation or issue, write a list of questions that will enable you to gather information needed to address the problem. |

| **Possible Solutions & Strategies** | **Workshops, seminars, and courses** |
|---|---|

_____

_____

_____

■ Check your district, regional service agency, state department, or colleges and universities in your area for opportunities for building capacity in this skill area.

**Mentor, coaches, and supervisors**

_____

_____

_____

**Ask:** Who can mentor me in this area and help me prioritize issues?
What are the questions I can ask a mentor about behavior and practice in this area?

■ Discuss the following with an administrative mentor: the kinds of school issues that need to be dealt with immediately, sensitive or potentially explosive situations and methods for handling them with caution, and situations which require communication with central office personnel.

■ Practice establishing priority rankings of problems and issues facing the school or district and discuss this ranking with a mentor.

**Readings** (see Appendix 5 for an extensive list)

Ackerman, R. H., Donaldson, G. A., & van der Bogert, R. (1996). *Making sense as a school leader: Persisting questions, creative opportunities*. San Francisco, CA: Jossey-Bass.

Black, J. A., & English, F. (1997). *What they don't tell you in schools of education about school administration*. Lanham, MD: Scarecrow Education Publishing.

Covey, S. R., Merrill, R. A., & Merrill, R. R. (1996). *First things first*. New York, NY: Free Press.

**Off-the-job development opportunities**

_____

_____

_____

What organizations and committees can I become active in to practice the behaviors?

**NASSP professional development opportunities**

■ Online courses

■ Seminars

■ Web-based resources

■ Customized professional development
(Visit www.principals.org/ProfessionalDevelopment.aspx to see current offerings.)

| | |
|---|---|
| **Assess Readiness & Build Capacity** | **Ask:** What do climate surveys, such as CASE from NASSP, tell me about the readiness and the capacity of the school community (faculty members, students, and parents) that will affect how and whether I should implement a solution? |
| | _____ |
| | Who will be affected by my personal development activities in this skill area? How? |
| | _____ |
| | What specific professional development in this skill area can I engage in that will have the greatest impact on my personal and professional capacity and the needs of the school? |
| | _____ |
| | What school data (e.g., achievement; attendance, graduation, and dropout rates; demographics; and instructional staff qualifications, experience, and background) affect my professional development needs and the possible solutions I identified above? How? |
| | _____ |
| **Create & Communicate Plan** | See page 109 to develop your plan. Ask: How will I share my personal learning plan with others? Specifically, how will I encourage every adult in my school to have a learning plan based on their developmental need in the context of the needs of the school and the students? |
| | _____ |
| **Implement Plan** | This is how I will practice the indicators to build capacity in the skill: |
| | _____ |

**Monitor & Adjust**

These are the specific measures of progress I will use in this skill area:

_____

_____

_____

These are the specific measures of progress I will use to determine the impact my progress in this area is having on the needs of the school:

_____

_____

_____

This is the feedback I will solicit: (when, from whom, in what form):

_____

_____

_____

I will use these aides to help in my development (e.g., reflection, journaling):

_____

_____

_____

Return to "Gather & Analyze Data" at the beginning of this instrument to establish new priorities within the same skill or to begin work on another skill.

## How Your Colleagues Put It in Action

Following are excerpts from interviews with several middle level and high school leaders related to **judgment**.

"Urgency issues come and go. Important issues usually stick around. I also try to never let myself be sucked into someone else's urgency—or their perception that it is urgent. I use this little test in my head before I make a commitment: Some things are urgent, some are important, some are urgent and important, and some are not urgent and not important."

—Ned Kirsch, Principal, Essex (VT) Middle School–Essex Town School District

"I had a rule: I wanted those most impacted by a decision to be a part of the process. Teachers should have input into key decisions that affect them and students should have the same voice in decisions that impact them. We were opening a new school and for the first time closing the campus and lunch. That meant a totally different daily schedule. I discussed the issue with our teacher leaders, and they suggested that we appoint a specific staff member to develop some alternative schedules. The teacher developed

10 different daily schedules. We discussed the merits of each and the teacher-leaders brought the recommendations to the general faculty for discussion and vote. The faculty voted 82% in favor of one schedule that happened to be the schedule recommended by the teacher leaders. I never heard one complaint about the schedule. I learned the hard way that trying to be benevolent and please my staff was not as effective as actually involving them in the decisions.

"Most decisions do not require an immediate response. So, we took as much time as we needed. We didn't procrastinate or creatively avoid deciding, but we intentionally consulted others to get another perspective. My judgment is fantastic when I rely on the collective intelligence of the staff. Consequently, we spent much less time cleaning up messes resulting from hasty decisions.

"One strategy that really worked well was the use of "debuggers." Software companies use debuggers to find out what is wrong with a software program. Every staff has someone who can find something wrong with every idea. Instead of fighting them, I utilized them. I would ask them if they were willing to be a sounding board when we needed to bounce ideas off of staff. They always agreed, and they always found something wrong with a proposal. I took their objections and resolved them in advance. So, when we proposed the ideas, they already had the blessing of the debugger. Over time, they became less and less critical and more and more constructive."

—Mel Riddile, NASSP

"I don't have all the answers. So here at Boaz Middle School, I'm the chief learner. I want to be out there on the cutting edge of learning new practices and new strategies. And I turn to research to discover what those best practices and strategies are—the strategies that will work, and that will be successful with our middle school students."

—Ray Landers, Principal, Boaz (AL) Middle School,
MetLife/NASSP 2009 National Middle Level Principal of the Year

"To involve more people in the school decision-making process I began by having open-agenda meetings. Basically, I dedicated time to talk one-on-one with each and every staff member. And then I opened it up to parents and students to really hear what was in their hearts about their school, what they felt about where the school was at the present time, and what they wanted the school to become.

"By looking at all of that information, we developed a vision of where our school could go and what our school could become. We developed a sense of team; we have student teams that have a voice in our school: we ask our students what they like about things, what they see that's working, what they see that is not working. We have the leadership council, we have the department chairs, grade-level team leaders, we have academic families or academic teams, and they all intermingle. We have a regular system of time that we allot and commit as a priority to share information and to share ideas so we all work together for student success."

—Delic Loyde, Principal, Stelle Claughton Middle School, Houston, TX,
a 2009 MetLife-NASSP Breakthrough School

**Activity #4**

To practice identification of behavioral indicators related to **judgment**, list the indicators that you saw in the actions of these school leaders.

| Behavioral Indicators Identified | Practice, Action, or Sentiment From Interviews |
| --- | --- |
|  |  |
|  |  |
|  |  |
|  |  |

## Skill: Results Orientation

**Defined:** Assuming responsibility. Recognizing when a decision is required. Taking prompt action as issues emerge. Resolving short-term issues while balancing them against long-term objectives.

Behavioral indicators of results orientation:

- Takes action to move issues toward closure
- Initiates action for improvement
- Determines the criteria that indicate a problem or issue is resolved
- Considers the implications of a decision before taking action
- Makes decisions on the basis of information
- Relates individual issues to the larger picture.

## How Do *You* Put It in Action?

### Activity #1

To begin to self assess your capacity in **results orientation**, reflect on what it looks like when you perform each of the behaviors. List some specific examples from your own practice as evidence that you can and do perform each behavior.

| Personal Reflection: My View | |
| --- | --- |
| **Behavior/descriptor** | **Give examples of your performance of this behavior and the frequency with which it occurs. Be specific.** |
| Takes action to move issues toward closure | |
| Initiates action for improvement | |
| Determines the criteria that indicate a problem or issue is resolved | |
| Considers the implications of a decision before taking action | |
| Makes decisions on the basis of information | |
| Relates individual issues to the larger picture | |

## Activity #2

Discuss **results orientation** and its indicators with your supervisor, mentor, or coach. Elicit feedback regarding your effectiveness in demonstrating these skills. Discuss strategies for practice that builds greater capacity.

| Feedback: View of a Colleague, Supervisor, Mentor, or Coach | | |
|---|---|---|
| **Behavior/descriptor** | **Effectiveness in demonstrating** | **Strategies to build capacity** |
| Takes action to move issues toward closure | | |
| Initiates action for improvement | | |
| Determines the criteria that indicate a problem or issue is resolved | | |
| Considers the implications of a decision before taking action | | |
| Makes decisions on the basis of additional information | | |

## Activity #3

Complete the following chart to assess your ability in this skill. You will use the results to develop your personal learning plan in Chapter 7.

| Results Orientation: How Do *You* Put It in Action? | |
| --- | --- |
| **Gather & Analyze Data** | **Ask:** How is my on-the-job performance in this skill area?<br><br>■ Reflect on my performance of the results orientation behavioral indicators—the frequency with which I engage in each behavior as opposed to my ability to perform the behavior.<br><br>■ Solicit face-to-face feedback from a variety of sources—such as a mentor, a coach, a supervisor, supervisees, and colleagues—that focuses on results orientation indicators.<br><br>■ Seek anonymous feedback from the 360-degree tool available from NASSP (www.principals.org).<br><br>■ Seek data from a formal assessment process (e.g., Selecting and Developing 21st Century Leaders and Leadership Skills Assessments from NASSP).<br><br>■ Review how I measure my performance on the indicators. Discuss results with mentor or colleague. |
| **Possible Solutions & Strategies** | Assignments that stretch and provide practice in this skill:<br><br>_____<br>_____<br>_____<br><br>■ Convene a committee or task force to study an issue regarding teaching and learning. Use a written charge that you have drafted for that group. In that charge, include the specific purpose and objectives for the group related to improved learning, the advisory or decision-making status of the group, resources that are available to assist in the group's work, to whom the group will report, your expectations, and deadlines or a timeline.<br><br>■ Develop strategies to challenge employees to bring a possible solution with every problem.<br><br>■ Explore and develop organizational techniques that incorporate setting priorities and timelines for actions or decisions.<br><br>■ Practice using a personal planning calendar or PDA. Practice setting deadlines for yourself and your staff. Use a tickler file to check your progress and the progress of others in meeting expectations and deadlines.<br><br>**Workshops, seminars, and courses**<br><br>_____<br>_____<br>_____<br><br>■ Check your district, regional service agency, state department, or colleges and universities in your area for opportunities for building capacity in this skill area. |

| **Possible Solutions & Strategies** | **Mentor, coaches, and supervisors** |
|---|---|
| | _____ |
| | _____ |
| | _____ |
| | **Ask:** Who can mentor me in this area and help me prioritize issues? What are the questions I can ask a mentor about behavior and practice in this area? |
| | ■ Discuss the following with an administrative mentor: the kinds of school issues that need to be dealt with immediately, sensitive or potentially explosive situations and methods for handling them with caution, and situations which require communication with central office personnel. |
| | ■ Practice establishing priority rankings of problems and issues facing the school or district and discuss this ranking with a mentor. |
| | **Readings** (see Appendix 5 for an extensive list) |
| | Ackerman, R. H., Donaldson, G. A., & van der Bogert, R. (1996). *Making sense as a school leader: Persisting questions, creative opportunities*. San Francisco, CA: Jossey-Bass. |
| | Black, J. A., & English, F. (1997). *What they don't tell you in schools of education about school administration*. Lanham, MD: Scarecrow Education Publishing. |
| | Covey, S. R., Merrill, R. A., & Merrill, R. R. (1996). *First things first*. New York, NY: Free Press. |
| | **Off-the-job development opportunities** |
| | _____ |
| | _____ |
| | _____ |
| | What organizations and committees can I become active in to practice the behaviors? |
| | **NASSP professional development opportunities** |
| | ■ Online courses |
| | ■ Seminars |
| | ■ Web-based resources |
| | ■ Customized professional development |
| | (Visit www.principals.org/ProfessionalDevelopment.aspx to see current offerings.) |

| **Assess Readiness & Build Capacity** | **Ask:** What do climate surveys, such as CASE from NASSP, tell me about the readiness and the capacity of the school community (faculty members, students, and parents) that will affect how and whether I implement a solution that I identified? |
| --- | --- |
| | _____ _____ _____ |
| | Who will be affected by my personal development activities in this skill area? How? |
| | _____ _____ _____ |
| | What specific development in this skill area can I engage in that will have the greatest impact on personal/professional capacity and the needs of the school? |
| | _____ _____ _____ |
| | What school data (e.g., achievement; attendance, graduation, and dropout rates; demographics; and instructional staff qualifications, experience, and background) affect my professional development needs and the possible solutions I identified? How? |
| | _____ _____ _____ |
| **Create & Communicate Plan** | See page 109 to develop your plan. Ask: How will I share my personal learning plan with others? |
| | _____ _____ _____ |
| | Specifically, how will I encourage every adult in my school to have a learning plan that is based on their developmental needs in the context of the needs of the school and the students? |
| | _____ _____ _____ |
| **Implement Plan** | This is how I will practice the indicators to build capacity in the skill: |
| | _____ _____ _____ |

| **Monitor & Adjust** | These are the specific measures of progress I will use in this skill area: |
| --- | --- |
| | _____ |
| | _____ |
| | _____ |
| | These are the specific measures of progress I will use to determine the impact my progress in this area is having on the needs of the school: |
| | _____ |
| | _____ |
| | _____ |
| | This is the feedback I will solicit: (when, from whom, in what form): |
| | _____ |
| | _____ |
| | _____ |
| | I will use these aids to help in my development (e.g., reflection, journaling): |
| | _____ |
| | _____ |
| | _____ |
| | Return to "Gather & Analyze Data" at the beginning of this instrument to establish new priorities within the same skill or to begin work on another skill. |

## How Your Colleagues Put It in Action

Below you will find excerpts from interviews with several middle level and high school leaders related to **results orientation**.

---

"Student learning is at the centerpiece of everything that we do. Each and everything that we do, we ask, what does it have to do with learning? As we begin to look at things, we need to establish a sense of urgency in order to change vision into reality. I think as you're changing it into reality, everything needs to be led by your leadership team. And you need to empower your quality teachers. You've got to have that collaborative atmosphere, and to let those really good teachers, those superstars, be empowered to make the changes and do the things that they need to do in order to show success to boys and girls.

"The power of collaboration [is that] it has to be a team effort. You've got to know how to involve people in the decision-making process, and how to make that decision-making process theirs. Through that, they have ownership of the process and then it becomes successful. They're the experts. Your teachers are the ones who are in the trenches each and every day. They know what's going to be best for the boys and girls in your school, so you have to empower that leadership team, and you have to permit them to lead."

—Ray Landers, Principal, Boaz (AL) Middle School,
MetLife/NASSP 2009 National Middle Level Principal of the Year

---

"The key for me here is making decisions on the basis of information. I learned that our school could not be led on intuition. Too often, intuition is wrong. Think about it. We are attempting to do what no one else has ever done—raise academic achievement for all students. Because no one has experience, we are pioneers, and we can't rely on guess-work and the past to inform us. We have to look at data, talk with experts, talk with staff members so that we make certain that we leave no stone unturned.

"We always set benchmarks for success and developed a roadmap for getting there. I told the staff that we had to spend as much time planning our school's future as they spent planning their vacation. We had to first decide where we wanted to go and then figure out the course to get there on time and within budget.

"We had a stated outcome for everything: 1300 lexile for all graduates, all trash off the cafeteria tables within 30 seconds after the bell rings, and all ninth graders graduate to tenth grade. Without a stated outcome, vision is hollow. In today's schools, activity does not equal success."

—Mel Riddile, NASSP

## Activity #4

To practice identifying behavioral indicators that are related to **results orientation**, list the indicators that you saw in the actions of these school leaders.

| Behavioral Indicators Identified | Practice, Action, or Sentiment From Interviews |
| --- | --- |
|  |  |
|  |  |
|  |  |
|  |  |

## Skill: Organizational Ability

**Defined:** Planning and scheduling one's own and the work of others so that resources are used appropriately. Scheduling flow of activities; establishing procedures to monitor projects. Practicing time and task management; knowing what to delegate and to whom.

Behavioral indicators of organizational ability:

- Delegates responsibilities to others
- Plans to monitor delegated responsibilities
- Develops action plans
- Monitors progress
- Establishes timelines, schedules, or milestones
- Prepares for meetings
- Uses available resources.

## How Do *You* Put It Into Action?

### Activity #1

To begin to self assess your capacity in **organizational ability**, reflect on what it looks like when you perform each of the behaviors. List some specific examples from your own practice as evidence that you can and do perform this behavior.

| Personal Reflection: My View | |
|---|---|
| **Behavior/descriptor** | **Give examples of your performance of this behavior and the frequency with which it occurs. Be specific.** |
| Delegates responsibilities to others | |
| Plans to monitor delegated responsibilities | |
| Develops action plans | |
| Monitors progress | |
| Establishes timelines, schedules, or milestones | |
| Prepares for meetings | |
| Uses available resources | |

**Activity #2**

Discuss **organizational ability** and its indicators with your supervisor, a mentor, or a coach. Elicit feedback regarding your effectiveness in demonstrating these skills. Discuss strategies for practice that builds greater capacity.

| Feedback: View of a Colleague, Supervisor, Mentor, or Coach | | |
|---|---|---|
| **Behavior/descriptor** | **Effectiveness in demonstrating** | **Strategies to build capacity** |
| Delegates responsibilities to others | | |
| Plans to monitor delegated responsibilities | | |
| Develops action plans | | |
| Monitors progress | | |
| Establishes timelines, schedules, or milestones | | |
| Prepares for meetings | | |
| Uses available resources | | |

## Activity #3

Complete the following chart to assess your ability in this skill. You will use the results to develop your personal learning plan in Chapter 7.

| Organizational Ability: How Do *You* Put It in Action? | |
|---|---|
| **Gather & Analyze Data** | **Ask:** How is my on-the-job performance in this skill area?<br><br>■ Reflect on your performance of the organizational ability behavioral indicators—the frequency with which you engage in each behavior as opposed to your ability to perform the behavior.<br><br>■ Solicit face-to-face feedback from a variety of sources—such as a mentor, a coach, a supervisor, supervisees, and colleagues—that focuses on the organizational ability indicators.<br><br>■ Seek anonymous feedback from the 360-degree tool available from NASSP (www.principals.org).<br><br>■ Seek data from a formal assessment process (e.g., Selecting and Developing 21st Century Leaders and Leadership Skills Assessments from NASSP).<br><br>■ Review your performance on the indicators. Discuss the results with a mentor or a colleague. |
| **Possible Solutions & Strategies** | Assignments that stretch and provide practice in this skill:<br><br>_____<br><br>_____<br><br>■ Discuss with an administrative mentor the organizational techniques that he or she has found to be effective in handling the complex task of balancing school management with instructional leadership.<br><br>■ Conduct an assessment of the culture in your school or district to determine the atmosphere for risk-taking, meeting needs, and the like, and along with your team, develop a plan to improve the culture as needed. Understand that culture is nurtured, not discovered.<br><br>■ Develop and use timelines for the completion of multiple or complex tasks.<br><br>■ Develop priority task lists with colleagues. Manage your tasks and those of others by setting objectives and prioritizing them in terms of time and importance as determined by your and the school's vision.<br><br>■ Practice delegating to others tasks that they can successfully accomplish to increase their sense of belonging and the accomplishment of members of a group. |

| **Possible Solutions & Strategies** | **Workshops, seminars, and courses** |
|---|---|

_____

_____

_____

_____

- Participate in seminars that deal with effective management, administrative effectiveness, and effective meetings.
- Participate in a workshop or seminar on strategic planning.
- Check your district, regional service agency, state department, or colleges and universities in your area for opportunities for building capacity in this skill area.

**Mentor, coaches, and supervisors**

_____

_____

_____

_____

**Ask:** Who can mentor me in this area and help me prioritize issues?

What are the questions I can ask a mentor about behavior and practice in this area?

- Discuss with a mentor the conditions and strategies for delegating tasks and for monitoring or following up on tasks that were delegated.
- Develop a mentor relationship with a trusted colleague who is known to be strong in organizational ability.

**Readings** (see Appendix 5 for an extensive list)

Blaydes, J. (2004). *Survival skills for the principalship: A treasure chest of time-savers, short-cuts, and strategies to help you keep a balance in your life.* Thousand Oaks, CA: Corwin.

Buck, F. (2008). *Get organized! Time management for school leaders.* Larchmont, NY: Eye on Education.

Fitzwater, I. (2001). *Time management for school administrators.* Rockport, MA: Pro-Active Publications.

**Off-the-job development opportunities**

_____

_____

_____

**Ask:** What organizations/committees can I become active in to practice the behaviors?

**NASSP professional development opportunities**

- Online courses
- Seminars
- Web-based resources
- Customized professional development

(Visit www.principals.org/ProfessionalDevelopment.aspx to see current offerings.)

| | |
|---|---|
| **Assess Readiness & Build Capacity** | **Ask:** What do climate surveys, such as CASE from NASSP, tell me about the readiness and the capacity of the school community (faculty members, students, and parents) that will affect how and whether I implement a solution?<br><br>_____<br>_____<br>_____<br><br>Who will be affected by my personal development activities in this skill area? How?<br><br>_____<br>_____<br>_____<br><br>What specific development in this skill area can I engage in that will have the greatest impact on personal/professional capacity and the needs of the school?<br><br>_____<br>_____<br>_____<br><br>What school data (e.g., achievement; attendance, graduation, and drop-out rates; demographics; and instructional staff qualifications, experience, and background) affect my professional development needs and the possible solutions I identified? How?<br><br>_____<br>_____<br>_____ |
| **Create & Communicate Plan** | See page 109 to develop your plan.<br>**Ask:** How will I share my personal learning plan with others?<br><br>_____<br>_____<br>_____<br><br>Specifically, how will I encourage every adult in my school to have a learning plan based on their developmental needs in the context of the needs of the school and the students?<br><br>_____<br>_____<br>_____ |
| **Implement Plan** | This is how I will practice the indicators to build capacity in the skill:<br><br>_____<br>_____<br>_____ |

| Monitor & Adjust | These are the specific measures of progress I will use in this skill area: |
|---|---|
| | _____ |
| | _____ |
| | _____ |
| | |
| | These are the specific measures of progress I will use to determine the impact my progress in this area is having on the needs of the school: |
| | _____ |
| | _____ |
| | _____ |
| | |
| | This is the feedback I will solicit: (when, from whom, in what form): |
| | _____ |
| | _____ |
| | _____ |
| | |
| | I will use these aids to help in my development (e.g., reflection, journaling): |
| | _____ |
| | _____ |
| | _____ |
| | |
| | Return to "Gather & Analyze Data" at the beginning of this instrument to establish new priorities within the same skill or to begin work on another skill. |

## How Your Colleagues Put It in Action

Following are excerpts from interviews with school leaders related to **organizational ability**.

"I always shared responsibility among my assistants and lead teachers. I believed in giving them a responsibility and then getting out of their way and letting them do their job. There is no way one person can do it all especially in today's schools. The leaders must have a system in place to monitor and check on job completion. We would meet on a set schedule weekly to check on tasks and progress of programs. I would avoid meeting just to meet, we utilized memos (e-mail) for items of information, and scheduled meetings when necessary, always with an agenda and time frames for each agenda item. We never left a meeting without assigning responsibilities and time frames for expected item completion.

"Everything is examined against what needs to be completed so we can accomplish our goals on a daily, weekly, and semester basis. The number one priority is making sure teachers have what is necessary for them to teach their students daily. Everything we do has to be good for kids, if not, we don't do it. Therefore, as items and emergencies come up, our first thought is how it will affect the learning for children and priorities are assigned to items on that basis."

—Santo Pino, retired principal, Naples, FL

"Whereas in the past, the principal needed to be a good manager, today principals need to be strong instructional leaders who are also good managers. In general, I focus most of my time on big picture, instructional tasks first. However, I cannot neglect the managerial tasks, which I attempt to delegate as much as possible. When "hot button" issues arise, they most always take precedence. In summary, instructional leadership is most important and always on my mind. It's the overview, with "hot button" situations and attention to managerial details taking priority as necessary."

—Terry Wolfson, Principal, Hopkins West Jr. High, Minnetonka, MN

"I answer e-mail whenever I sit down at my desk; I never let them pile up. I answer every phone call I get immediately. If I need to read, I duck into a classroom during students' half-hour silent reading time. This allows me to be seen as learner by the students, but it also gives me some real quality uninterrupted reading time. I also delegate responsibility and have trust in those I ask to take on that work. I also fully realize that everything will not get done and that I have my own family life. Tomorrow is always another opportunity."

—Ned Kirsch, Principal, Essex (VT) Middle School–Essex Town School District

## Activity #4

To practice identifying the behavioral indicators related to **organizational ability**, list the indicators that you saw in the actions of this school leader.

| Behavioral Indicators Identified | Practice, Action, or Sentiment From Interviews |
|---|---|
|  |  |
|  |  |
|  |  |
|  |  |

## Reference

National Association of Secondary School Principals. (2009). *Breaking ranks: A field guide for leading change.* Reston, VA: Author.

# 5 Communication

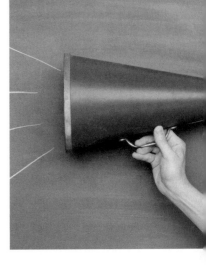

*The two words "information" and "communication" are often used interchangeably, but they signify quite different things. Information is giving out, communication is getting through.*

—*Sydney J. Harris*

Oral Communication ■ Written Communication

Advertisements, press releases, copywriters, communications directors—why is it that so much in the way of personnel and resources is allocated to communication in the business world? Because the message matters! Companies, political campaigns, bond offerings, and school initiatives flourish or fail based on "what gets through"—not on how much information is put out.

How many times has an excellent plan been shelved because the communication about the plan was premature, outdated, or ineffective? Your role as a school leader is to ensure that your own communications as well as those of others on your team bring about the desired results. A quick Internet search will deliver many studies and quotes from leadership gurus about the importance of communication. But despite the emphasis on communication in world and personal events, people continue to repeat the same mistakes by ignoring sage advice and failing to practice communication skills. Consequently, when those skills are needed most, the skills have not been properly cultivated to have the desired impact.

## Behaviors Associated With Communication

Generally speaking, knowing your audience is crucial to any communication. What unique characteristics do the people you are trying to reach possess? What prior knowledge of the topic do they have? Taking the time to discover how others perceive your communication—in one-on-one settings; in group discussions; and in your written communications such as newsletters, memos and e-mails—is well worth your time. Understanding whether or not your communications are simply filed away or have an impact on the audience is essential for you to know immediately—not to find out later when the clarity and effectiveness of your communication matters the most and others discover your communication skills to be lacking. A steady stream of ineffective communication will have the same affect as the boy who cried wolf.

By systematically seeking the input of a wide variety of others to assess your communication, you demonstrate that you value their insights into one of the most important things that you do as a school leader—communicate. Simply asking for input and then acting upon it is a valuable team building activity that will

- Build your credibility
- Establish your position as a leader of people who are interested in learning
- Demonstrate that you are not afraid of feedback.

Each of the next two sections will discuss a skill as well as behavioral indicators that can be analyzed and practiced. It is important to break each of these skills into discrete components (behavioral indicators) that help you analyze your own performance. To help you to understand the concepts more fully and conduct your self-analysis methodically, each skill section is divided into four subsections:

- A definition of the term
- Behavioral indicators and descriptors of practice
- Personal development tools and activities that can help you practice the skill to build capacity and greater effectiveness
- Examples of other school leaders putting the behaviors in action.

## Skill: Oral Communication

**Defined:** Clearly communicating. Making oral presentations that are clear and easy to understand.

Behavioral indicators of oral communication:

- Demonstrates effective presentation skills
- Speaks articulately
- Uses proper grammar, pronunciation, diction, and syntax
- Tailors messages to meet the needs of unique audiences
- Clearly presents thoughts and ideas in one-on-one, small-group, and formal presentation settings.

---

*If I am to speak ten minutes, I need a week for preparation; if fifteen minutes, three days; if half an hour, two days; if an hour, I am ready now.*

—Woodrow Wilson

---

# How Do *You* Put It in Action?

## Activity #1

To begin to self assess your capacity in **oral communication**, reflect on what it looks like when you perform each of the behaviors. List some specific examples from your own practice that serve as evidence that you can and do perform this behavior.

| Personal Reflection: My View | |
| --- | --- |
| **Behavior/descriptor** | **Give examples of your performance of this behavior and the frequency with which it occurs. Be specific.** |
| Demonstrates effective presentation skills | |
| Speaks articulately | |
| Uses proper grammar, pronunciation, diction, and syntax | |
| Tailors messages to meet the needs of unique audiences | |
| Clearly presents thoughts and ideas in one-on-one, small-group, and formal presentation settings | |
| Uses available resources | |

## Activity #2

Discuss **oral communication** and its indicators with your supervisor, mentor, or coach. Elicit feedback regarding your effectiveness in demonstrating these skills. Discuss strategies for practice that builds greater capacity.

| Feedback: View of a Colleague, Supervisor, Mentor, or Coach | | |
| --- | --- | --- |
| **Behavior/descriptor** | **Effectiveness in demonstrating** | **Strategies to build capacity** |
| Demonstrates effective presentation skills | | |
| Speaks articulately | | |
| Uses proper grammar, pronunciation, diction, and syntax | | |
| Tailors messages to meet the needs of unique audiences | | |
| Clearly presents thoughts and ideas in one-on-one, small-group, and formal presentation settings | | |

## Activity #3

Complete the following chart to assess your ability in this skill. You will use the results to develop your personal learning plan in Chapter 7.

| Oral Communication: How Do *You* Put It in Action? | |
| --- | --- |
| **Gather & Analyze Data** | **Ask:** How is my on-the-job performance in this skill area?<br>■ Reflect on your performance of the oral communication behavioral indicators—the frequency with which you engage in each behavior as opposed to your ability to perform the behavior.<br>■ Solicit face-to-face feedback from a variety of sources—such as a mentor, a coach, a supervisor, supervisees, and colleagues—that focuses on the oral communication indicators.<br>■ Seek anonymous feedback from the 360-degree tool available from NASSP (www.principals.org).<br>■ Seek data from a formal assessment process (e.g., Selecting and Developing 21st Century Leaders and Leadership Skills Assessments from NASSP).<br>■ Review your performance on the indicators. Discuss the results with a mentor or a colleague. |

| **Possible Solutions & Strategies** | Assignments that stretch and provide practice in this skill: |
|---|---|
| | _____ |
| | _____ |
| | _____ |
| | ■ When communicating expectations (orally or in writing), be specific about the desired process or product. For example, when appointing a committee, indicate the task or purpose, timelines, and type of action needed. |
| | ■ Make presentations to groups within the school and district as frequently as possible. Seek feedback regarding voice quality (tone, volume, rate of speaking, and clarity), the use of appropriate presentation devices (organization of thoughts, use of visual aids, use of organizers, vocal inflection, use of correct grammar and pronunciation, use of gestures and positive body language, and appropriate eye contact), and the content of the presentation. |
| | **Workshops, seminars, and courses** |
| | _____ |
| | _____ |
| | _____ |
| | ■ Participate in programs, workshops, and seminars that are designed to develop skills in effective oral communication and public speaking. |
| | ■ Check your district, regional service agency, state department, or colleges and universities in your area for opportunities for building capacity in this skill area. |
| | **Mentor, coaches, and supervisors** |
| | _____ |
| | _____ |
| | _____ |
| | **Ask:** Who can mentor me in this area and help me prioritize issues? |
| | ■ What are the questions I can ask a mentor about behavior and practice in this area? |
| | ■ Videotape some of the presentations you make and evaluate them for oral communication effectiveness. Ask a mentor or colleague to assist you in your evaluation. |
| | ■ Ask a mentor or trusted colleague for feedback regarding organization of thoughts in impromptu oral presentations. |
| | **Readings** (see Appendix 5 for an extensive list) |
| | Garmston, R. & Wellman, B. (1992). *How to make presentations that teach and transform.* Alexandria, VA: ASCD. |
| | Lemay, E. & Schwamberger, J. (2007). *Listen up!: How to communicate effectively at work.* Santa Cruz, CA: Papilio. |

| | |
|---|---|
| **Possible Solutions & Strategies** | **Off-the-job development opportunities** <br><br>_____ <br>_____ <br>_____ <br><br>**Ask:** What organizations and committees can I become active in to practice the behaviors? Join Toastmasters or a similar organization that promotes the development of public speaking skills. <br><br>**NASSP professional development opportunities** <br>■ Online courses <br>■ Seminars <br>■ Web-based resources <br>■ Customized professional development <br>(Visit www.principals.org/ProfessionalDevelopment.aspx to see current offerings.) |
| **Assess Readiness & Build Capacity** | **Ask:** What do climate surveys, such as CASE from NASSP, tell me about readiness and capacity of the school community (faculty members, students, and parents) that will affect how and whether I implement a solution? <br><br>_____ <br>_____ <br>_____ <br><br>Who will be affected by my personal development activities in this skill area? How? <br><br>_____ <br>_____ <br>_____ <br><br>What specific development in this skill area can I engage in that will have the greatest impact on personal/professional capacity and the needs of the school? <br><br>_____ <br>_____ <br>_____ <br><br>What school data (e.g., achievement; attendance, graduation, and drop-out rates; demographics; and instructional staff qualifications, experience, and background) affect my professional development needs and the possible solutions I identified? How? <br><br>_____ <br>_____ <br>_____ |

| **Oral Communication: How Do *You* Put It in Action?** |
|---|

| | |
|---|---|
| **Create & Communicate Plan** | See page 109 to develop your plan.<br>**Ask:** How will I share my personal learning plan with others?<br><br>_____<br>_____<br>_____<br><br>Specifically, how will I encourage every adult in my school to have a learning plan based on their developmental needs in the context of the needs of the school and the students?<br><br>_____<br>_____<br>_____ |
| **Implement Plan** | This is how I will practice the indicators to build capacity in the skill:<br><br>_____<br>_____<br>_____ |
| **Monitor & Adjust** | These are the specific measures of progress I will use in this skill area:<br><br>_____<br>_____<br>_____<br><br>These are the specific measures of progress I will use to determine the impact my progress in this area is having on the needs of the school:<br><br>_____<br>_____<br>_____<br><br>This is the feedback I will solicit: (when, from whom, in what form):<br><br>_____<br>_____<br>_____<br><br>I will use these aids to help in my development (e.g., reflection, journaling):<br><br>_____<br>_____<br>_____<br><br>Return to "Gather & Analyze Data" at the beginning of this instrument to establish new priorities within the same skill or to begin work on another skill. |

## How Your Colleagues Put It in Action

Following you will find excerpts from interviews with school leaders related to **oral communication**.

---

"Besides the PTO, I met with a group of business partners on a quarterly basis to discuss what was happening at the school and the plans that were taking shape for the school improvement for the next school year. I avoided asking for money; we spent time on items that they could assist on that were not money items. Mentoring and assistance with reading and math were items that business partners often became involved with. As programs evolved, assistance of a monetary nature usually was provided by the partners who would often sponsor activities or projects they became involved with."

—Santo Pino, retired principal, Tampa, FL

---

"I live by the premise that I don't want surprises for any of our stakeholders. In the area of communication, I believe more is better and timeliness is crucial! We have used a variety of technologies to communicate with families where parents are given virtual snapshots into what is occurring in the classrooms. Moodle sites, group e-mails, and parent portals have not only allowed teachers to share the exciting learning activities occurring in their classrooms but have been a wonderful way to solicit parent interest in various volunteer opportunities in classrooms and school activities. When parents are informed of the exciting activities their children are experiencing, they become great ambassadors in the community. In our school community, families no longer have to rely on the usual adolescent response to, "What did you do in school today?" In addition, communication tools such as Connect Ed allow phone blitzes to families about special events and circumstances."

—Terry Wolfson, Principal, Hopkins West Jr. High, Minnetonka, MN

## Activity #4

To practice identifying behavioral indicators related to **oral communication**, list the indicators that you saw in the actions of this school leader.

| Behavioral Indicators Identified | Practice, Action, or Sentiment From Interviews |
| --- | --- |
| | |
| | |
| | |
| | |

## Skill: Written Communication

**Defined:** Expressing ideas clearly in writing; demonstrating technical proficiency. Writing appropriately for different audiences.

Behavioral indicators of written communication:

- Writes concisely
- Demonstrates technical proficiency in writing
- Expresses ideas clearly in writing
- Writes appropriately for different audiences.

## How Do *You* Put It in Action?

### Activity #1

To begin to self assess your capacity in **written communication**, reflect on what it looks like when you perform each of the behaviors. List some specific examples from your own practice as evidence that you can and do perform each behavior.

| Personal Reflection: My View | |
|---|---|
| **Behavior/descriptor** | **Give examples of your performance of this behavior and the frequency with which it occurs. Be specific.** |
| Writes concisely | |
| Demonstrates technical proficiency in writing | |
| Expresses ideas clearly in writing | |
| Writes appropriately for different audiences | |

## Activity #2

Discuss **written communication** and its indicators with your supervisor, mentor, or coach. Elicit feedback regarding your effectiveness in demonstrating these skills. Discuss strategies for practice that builds greater capacity.

| Feedback: View of a Colleague, Supervisor, Mentor, or Coach | | |
|---|---|---|
| **Behavior/descriptor** | **Effectiveness in demonstrating** | **Strategies to build capacity** |
| Writes concisely | | |
| Demonstrates technical proficiency in writing | | |
| Expresses ideas clearly in writing | | |
| Writes appropriately for different audiences | | |

## Activity #3

Complete the following chart to assess your ability in this skill. You will use the results to develop your personal learning plan in Chapter 7.

| Written Communication: How Do *You* Put It in Action? | |
|---|---|
| **Gather & Analyze Data** | **Ask:** How is my on-the-job performance in this skill area?<br>■ Reflect on my performance of the written communication behavioral indicators—the frequency with which I engage in each behavior as opposed to my ability to perform the behavior.<br>■ Solicit face-to-face feedback from a variety of sources—such as a mentor, a coach, a supervisor, supervisees, and colleagues—that focuses on the written communication indicators.<br>■ Seek anonymous feedback from the 360-degree tool available from NASSP (www.principals.org).<br>■ Seek data from a formal assessment process (e.g., Selecting and Developing 21st Century Leaders and Leadership Skills Assessments from NASSP).<br>■ Review how I measure my performance on the indicators. Discuss results with mentor or colleague. |

| | |
|---|---|
| **Possible Solutions & Strategies** | Assignments that stretch and provide practice in this skill: |

- When communicating expectations (orally or in writing), be specific about the desired process or product. For example, when appointing a committee, indicate the task or purpose, timelines and type of action needed.
- Establish a "buddy system" with a trusted colleague to ensure that correspondence is proofread prior to transmittal.
- Use a dictionary, style manual, and thesaurus when writing documents to be read by others.
- Volunteer to prepare press releases, news bulletins, program descriptions, grant proposals, and other documents for the school or district. Seek feedback from a mentor or trusted colleague regarding correctness and effectiveness of written communication.

**Workshops, seminars, and courses**

- Check your district, regional service agency, state department, or colleges and universities in your area for opportunities for building capacity in this skill area.

**Mentor, coaches, and supervisors**

**Ask:** Who can mentor me in this area and help me prioritize issues?

- What are the questions I can ask a mentor about behavior and practice in this area?
- Videotape some of the presentations you make and evaluate them for oral communication effectiveness. Ask a mentor or colleague to assist you in your evaluation.
- Ask a mentor or trusted colleague for feedback regarding your written communications.

**Readings** (see Appendix 5 for an extensive list)
Bates, J. D. (2000). *Writing with precision: How to write so that you cannot possibly be misunderstood.* New York, NY: Penguin Group.

Booher, D. (2009). *Booher's rules of business grammar: 101 fast and easy ways to correct the most common errors.* New York, NY: McGraw-Hill.

**Off-the-job development opportunities**

- What organizations and committees can I become active in to practice the behaviors?

| | |
|---|---|
| **Possible Solutions & Strategies** | **NASSP professional development opportunities**<br>■ Online courses<br>■ Seminars<br>■ Web-based resources<br>■ Customized professional development<br>(Visit www.principals.org/ProfessionalDevelopment.aspx to see current offerings.) |
| **Assess Readiness & Build Capacity** | What do climate surveys, such as CASE from NASSP, tell me about the readiness and the capacity of the school community (faculty members, students, and parents) that will affect how and whether I implement a solution?<br>_____<br>_____<br>_____<br><br>Who will be affected by my personal development activities in this skill area? How?<br>_____<br>_____<br>_____<br><br>What specific development in this skill area can I engage in that will have the greatest impact on my personal and professional capacity and the needs of the school?<br>_____<br>_____<br>_____<br><br>What school data (e.g., achievement; attendance, graduation, and drop-out rates; demographics; and instructional staff qualifications, experience, and background) affect my professional development needs and the possible solutions I identified? How?<br>_____<br>_____<br>_____ |
| **Create & Communicate Plan** | See page 109 to develop your plan.<br>**Ask:** How will I share my personal learning plan with others?<br>_____<br>_____<br>_____<br><br>Specifically, how will I encourage every adult in my school to have a learning plan based on their developmental needs in the context of the needs of the school and the students?<br>_____<br>_____<br>_____ |

## Written Communication: How Do *You* Put It in Action?

| | |
|---|---|
| **Implement Plan** | This is how I will practice the indicators to build capacity in the skill:<br><br>_____<br>_____<br>_____ |
| **Monitor & Adjust** | These are the specific measures of progress I will use in this skill area:<br><br>_____<br>_____<br>_____<br><br>These are the specific measures of progress I will use to determine the impact my progress in this area is having on the needs of the school:<br><br>_____<br>_____<br>_____<br><br>This is the feedback I will solicit: (when, from whom, in what form):<br><br>_____<br>_____<br>_____<br><br>I will use these aids to help in my development (e.g., reflection, journaling):<br><br>_____<br>_____<br>_____<br><br>Return to "Gather & Analyze Data" at the beginning of this instrument to establish new priorities within the same skill or to begin work on another skill. |

## How Your Colleagues Put It in Action

Following you will find excerpts from interviews with school leaders related to **written communication**.

---

"We have created a parent e-mail database that parents sign up on their own via our Web site or in our computer labs during back-to-school night. Our parents seem to most appreciate a quick e-mail about something small that they might never have heard about, for example, the developmental stage of middle schoolers. We also send out mass phone messages to parents.

"E-mail, the school Web site, and district meetings are the key tools of communication with the district. The community is consistently referred to our Web site for any info they could possibly want about our school. We work diligently to keep the site updated. Our headlines section carries news about student accomplishments, PTO activities, parent opportunities, even FAQs for rising sixth graders and their parents. We work closely with our feeder school and meet quarterly with our cluster schools.

"Students receive timely info via our live morning announcements. Those announcements are posted on our Web site, and scrolled on TV monitors during lunch. Students receive a daily "character" message from me with a closing line: "This is Mrs. K. reminding you to choose wisely today; use your mind as well as your heart."

—Janice Koslowski, Principal, Potomac Falls High School, Sterling, VA

---

"I wrote a weekly instructionally focused newsletter—about 35 a year—for many years. Each issue was between 1,200 and 1,500 words. Having the entire English department grade my newsletter was, at first, a bit intimidating, but I earned readership and the respect of my staff. Eventually, I had the entire school board, the mayor, central office staff, city council, and other principals on my distribution list. The culture in our school changed, in large part, as the result of consistent written communications."

—Mel Riddile, NASSP

## Activity #4

To practice identifying the behavioral indicators related to **written communication**, list the indicators that you saw in the actions of this school leader.

| Behavioral Indicators Identified | Practice, Action, or Sentiment From Interviews |
|---|---|
|  |  |
|  |  |
|  |  |

# 6 Developing Self and Others

*The great composer does not set to work because he is inspired,*
*but becomes inspired because he is working.*

—*Ernest Newman*

Developing Others ■ Understanding Own Strengths
and Weaknesses

A student's display of intellectual curiosity or an outstanding performance, an enthusiastic and engaging teacher, student leaders involved in a substantive debate about a pressing community concern—these are the work of the school leader. They are what inspires a principal, an assistant principal, or a teacher leader. Ensuring that these are not isolated events but that they occur every minute of every day in every classroom or activity is the challenge. How do you, as a school leader, develop the skills to ensure that it happens? How do you help others develop the skills to ensure that it happens?

Glenn Pethel (personal communication, July 9, 2009) of the Gwinnett County Public Schools believes the answer lies in leverage:

"The Greek mathematician Archimedes is credited with the statement, "Give me a lever long enough and I can move the world." Everyone involved in managing human capital continually seeks those levers that will move organizations forward. In the private sector, the progress is evidenced in greater profit and organizational efficacy. In education, the progress must be viewed as the advancement of student achievement. With human resources costs totaling more than 85% of most school district budgets, identifying and using those levers that effectively develop the skills of teachers and school leaders are vitally important. The NASSP Assessment Center process has been an effective lever for developing leaders for our schools. Gwinnett has used this approach to assessment and selection for more than two decades. Early identification of strengths and weaknesses has enabled the district to precisely and reliably target areas for development. Data from assessment center reports provide a clear and concise guide to selecting and developing leaders for schools of the 21st century."

In practice, this means that the principals, assistant principals, and teacher leaders are the levers to encourage schoolwide progress rather than pockets of progress. For those levers to be able to "move the school" by developing others they must first understand their own strengths and weaknesses that might hinder or enhance that effort. Each leader must ask: How can I develop my own skills enough to allow me to inspire others to do the same?

Effective leaders understand that leadership is a group of skills to be shared, not hoarded. Anyone who does not share these skills in a mentoring or coaching capacity is not leveraging resources—and may diminish his or her effectiveness as a leader. In the context of instructional leadership your primary role as a principal, assistant principal, or teacher leader is to mentor others. But doing so requires more than a pep talk every quarter or a quick critique of a lesson plan or reliance on the belief that the great people you hired should be left alone to do what they do best. Every principal, assistant principal, and teacher needs to develop and sustain a mentoring relationship. Without it, the levers of skill and experience are lost.

Losing that experience and skill is a challenge for schools. In a recent study of Texas schools, Fuller (2007) concluded that "principal stability impacts teacher retention, teacher quality, school culture/working conditions, and student achievement" and that "leadership behaviors can improve teacher working conditions, improve teacher retention, and improve student achievement" (slide 35).

Despite the importance of principals, Fuller (2007) found that the percentage of principals returning to a school after five years is also decreasing. This in turn leads to a higher degree of instability. Aspiring and existing principals and mentors can add to the stability by taking control of their own development.

## Behaviors Associated with Developing Self and Others

As the saying goes, there are two sides to every coin. You believe that you are deliberative; others believe you can't make a timely decision. You consider yourself decisive; others believe you shoot from the hip and use poor judgment. You believe you strive to develop others; others believe they are completely dependent on your every thought or pronouncement. You believe you are a proponent of teamwork; others believe all decisions are made at the top and trickle down.

The truth may lie somewhere in the middle, but because the stakes and your credibility are so important, wouldn't you rather have some basis upon which to form the conclusion that there is nothing you can do about the perception of others? When your career and the performance of so many students relies on your capacity for leadership, don't you owe it to yourself and others to know how strong your leadership really is—and how you can improve it? True leadership demands it.

The next two sections will discuss skills and behavioral indicators that can be analyzed and practiced. It is important to break each of these skills into discrete components (behavioral indicators and descriptors of practice) that better allow you to analyze your own performance. To help you to understand the concepts more fully and conduct that self-analysis methodically, each skill is divided into four subsections:

- A definition of the term
- Behavioral indicators and descriptors of practice
- Personal development tools and activities that can help you practice the skill to build capacity and effectiveness
- Examples of other school leaders putting the behaviors in action.

## Skill: Developing Others

**Defined:** Teaching, coaching, and helping others. Providing specific feedback based on observations and data.

Behavioral indicators of developing self and others:

- Shares expertise gained through experience
- Encourages others to change behaviors that inhibit professional growth
- Recommends specific developmental strategies
- Asks others for their perceptions of their professional development needs
- Seeks agreement on specific actions to be taken for developmental growth.

## How Do *You* Put It in Action?

### Activity #1

To begin to self assess your capacity in **developing others**, reflect on what it looks like when you perform each of the behaviors. List some specific examples from your own practice as evidence that you can and do perform each behavior.

| Personal Reflection: My View | |
| --- | --- |
| **Behavior/descriptor** | **Give examples of your performance of this behavior and the frequency with which it occurs. Be specific.** |
| Shares expertise gained through experience | |
| Encourages others to change behaviors that inhibit professional growth | |
| Recommends specific developmental strategies | |
| Asks others for their perceptions of their professional development needs | |
| Seeks agreement on specific actions to be taken for developmental growth | |

**Activity #2**

Discuss **developing others** and its indicators with your supervisor, mentor, or coach. Elicit feedback regarding your effectiveness in demonstrating these skills. Discuss strategies for practice that builds greater capacity.

| Feedback: View of a Colleague, Supervisor, Mentor, or Coach | | |
| --- | --- | --- |
| **Behavior/descriptor** | **Effectiveness in demonstrating** | **Strategies to build capacity** |
| Shares expertise gained through experience | | |
| Encourages others to change behaviors that inhibit professional growth | | |
| Recommends specific developmental strategies | | |
| Asks others for their perceptions of their professional development needs | | |
| Seeks agreement on specific actions to be taken for developmental growth | | |

**Activity #3**

Complete the following chart to assess your ability in this skill. You will use the results to develop your personal learning plan in Chapter 7.

| Developing Others: How Do *You* Put It in Action? | |
|---|---|
| **Gather & Analyze Data** | **Ask:** How is my on-the-job performance in this skill area?<br>■ Reflect on my performance of the developing others behavioral indicators—the frequency with which I engage in each behavior as opposed to my ability to perform the behavior.<br>■ Solicit face-to-face feedback from a variety of sources—such as a mentor, a coach, a supervisor, supervisees, and colleagues—that focuses on the developing self and others indicators.<br>■ Seek anonymous feedback from the 360-degree tool available from NASSP (www.principals.org).<br>■ Seek data from a formal assessment process (e.g., Selecting and Developing 21st Century Leaders and Leadership Skills Assessments from NASSP).<br>■ Review how I measure my performance on the indicators. Discuss results with mentor or colleague. |
| **Possible Solutions & Strategies** | Assignments that stretch and provide practice in this skill:<br>■ Practice identifying the strengths of others. Assign or delegate to them tasks that develop those strengths.<br>■ Seek leadership responsibility for groups assigned to accomplish specific tasks. Practice delegating tasks and responsibilities to group members. Develop procedures for monitoring work delegated and for providing feedback.<br>■ Develop a rotating leadership team for your school (department chairpersons or grade level chairs) that meets regularly to address issues, to provide communication from specific areas of campus, and to provide feedback to the principal.<br>■ Discuss with colleagues ways to model change for your staff.<br>■ Evaluate your organizational structure focusing on providing maximum opportunity for each staff member to contribute to the success of the school.<br>■ Identify staff members who are initiators and innovators. Give them opportunities (both large and small) to be leaders<br>■ Make a list of major activities, such as SIC, PTO, Strategic Planning, Booster Club, etc. Identify cochairpersons or assistant group leaders who are staff members to assume responsibility for the task under your leadership.<br>■ Organize a study group to focus on an area that you have identified as a need for additional professional development. Invite two or three others on your staff to join you in an in-depth study of this concern. Meet regularly to share ideas and concepts gained from your reading or investigation.<br>■ Practice making behaviorally specific notes while observing an individual or group. Deliver the feedback, focusing on behavior demonstrated.<br>■ Seek feedback from staff as to the value of support they have received in designing and evaluating their own individualized professional development plans. |

| | |
|---|---|
| **Possible Solutions & Strategies** | **Workshops, seminars, and courses** |

_____

_____

_____

- Participate in programs, workshops, and seminars that are designed to build skill in observing behavior and delivering feedback to others.
- Check your district, regional service agency, state department, or colleges and universities in your area for opportunities for building capacity in this skill area.

**Mentor, coaches, and supervisors**

_____

_____

_____

**Ask:** Who can mentor me in this area and help me prioritize issues?

- What are the questions I can ask a mentor about behavior and practice in this area?
- Work with a mentor or colleague who is skilled in designing strategies for motivating staff to improve instructional effectiveness.

**Readings** (see Appendix XX for an extensive list)

Crowther, F., Ferguson, M., & Hand, L. (2008). *Developing teacher leaders: How teacher leadership enhances school success*, Second Edition. Thousand Oaks, CA: Corwin/NASSP.

Stone, D. F., Patton, B., & Heen, S. (2000). *Difficult conversations: How to discuss what matters most*. New York, NY: Penguin.

**Off-the-job development opportunities**

_____

_____

_____

- What organizations and committees can I become active in to practice the behaviors?

**NASSP professional development opportunities**

- Online courses
- Seminars
- Web-based resources
- Customized professional development

(Visit www.principals.org/ProfessionalDevelopment.aspx to see current offerings.)

| **Developing Others: How Do *You* Put It in Action?** | |
|---|---|
| **Assess Readiness & Build Capacity** | **Ask:** What do climate surveys, such as CASE from NASSP, tell me about the readiness and the capacity of the school community (faculty members, students, and parents) that will affect how and whether I implement a solution? <br><br> _____ <br> _____ <br> _____ <br><br> Who will be affected by my personal development activities in this skill area? How? <br><br> _____ <br> _____ <br> _____ <br><br> What specific development in this skill area can I engage in that will have the greatest impact on my personal and professional capacity and the needs of the school? <br><br> _____ <br> _____ <br> _____ <br><br> What school data (e.g., achievement; attendance, graduation, and drop-out rates; demographics; and instructional staff qualifications, experience, and background) affect my professional development needs and the possible solutions I identified above? How? <br><br> _____ <br> _____ <br> _____ |
| **Create & Communicate Plan** | See page 109 to develop your plan. <br> **Ask:** How will I share my personal learning plan with others? <br><br> _____ <br> _____ <br> _____ <br><br> Specifically how will I encourage every adult in my school to have a learning plan based on their developmental needs in the context of the needs of the school and the students? <br><br> _____ <br> _____ <br> _____ |
| **Implement Plan** | This is how I will practice the indicators to build capacity in the skill: <br><br> _____ <br> _____ <br> _____ |

| Developing Others: How Do *You* Put It in Action? | |
|---|---|
| **Monitor & Adjust** | These are the specific measures of progress I will use in this skill area:<br><br>_____<br>_____<br>_____<br><br>These are the specific measures of progress I will use to determine the impact my progress in this area is having on the needs of the school:<br><br>_____<br>_____<br>_____<br><br>This is the feedback I will solicit: (when, from whom, in what form):<br><br>_____<br>_____<br>_____<br><br>I will use these aids to help in my development (e.g., reflection, journaling):<br><br>_____<br>_____<br>_____<br><br>Return to "Gather & Analyze Data" at the beginning of this instrument to establish new priorities within the same skill or to begin work on another skill. |

## How Your Colleagues Put It in Action

Below you will find excerpts from interviews with several middle level and high school leaders related to **developing others**.

---

"I was fortunate as an assistant principal that the principal gave me a lot of autonomy in my role. As long as what I wanted to try fit in with the direction the school was headed and I was willing to accept the responsibility for 'less than wonderful' results, I was given a lot of freedom to try things. One time I organized a middle school conference at our school during a regular school day. We had lots of visitors from other schools, and we worked around teacher prep times to let them present mini-workshops. Other teachers did demonstration lessons…it was a big success. We used the money we made from the registration fees to help us attend a national middle school conference that was held 300 miles away from us. I was able to work with the district administration and the school board to get a couple of extra in-service days in the calendar so we didn't have to hire subs. "It was a wonderful experience for the staff (and we repeated it about 7–8 years later when the conference returned to the state).

I guess these experiences shifted me into using the 'ask forgiveness, not permission' mode, and when the staff sees you operating like that, they tend to follow your lead, so I think I gave my teachers a lot of autonomy as well. As long as their plans and ideas were within the parameters of our school's vision and direction and I was kept informed of what folks were trying to do, I didn't necessarily require my staff to get permission to try new things.

"When I was named Principal of the Year in 2003, one of my teachers was quoted as saying that I gave 'teachers the latitude they need to use their own style in presenting the information to students. We know we have to give the ABCs, but how you cover them is up to the individual teacher,' she said. 'She has allowed us a lot of freedom to design our own curriculums.'"

—Patti Kinney, NASSP

"One of the best things you can help teachers appreciate is that you want feedback and you want them to give each other feedback…all outside of any formal evaluation system. So much of the focus in preparation programs is on students rather than how to work with teacher leaders and planning for adult learning and how best to work with adults. Some of the most important things we can help our peers do is to learn how to gather data about themselves, to understand reflection, and to trust people to give feedback, working with them to catch themselves doing a certain action or behavior and addressing one or two skills at a time.

"One of the things I've found is that new principals might not be as open and honest with a seasoned principal as they are with a person in the same boat (i.e., a new principal) because they aren't quite confident enough. So sometimes it's good to also have a confidante that understands your position.

"The good thing about working with less experienced leaders is that I am constantly re-assessing my own skills as I observe them and work with them to try different behaviors and skills. Each of the behaviors is something you can do and be seen doing. The simulations also give you a different perspective—allowing teacher leaders or principals to be put in different positions, for example being put in a different position such as supervisor of principals."

—Morgan Lee, Education Associates,
South Carolina Department of Education, Columbia

## Activity #4

To practice identifying the behavioral indicators that are related to **developing others**, list the indicators that you saw in the actions of these school leaders.

| Behavioral Indicators Identified | Practice, Action, or Sentiment From Interviews |
|---|---|
| | |
| | |
| | |
| | |

## Skill: Understanding Your Own Strengths and Weaknesses

**Defined:** Identifying personal strengths and weaknesses. Taking responsibility for improvement by actively pursuing developmental activities. Striving for continuous learning.

Behavioral indicators of understanding own strengths and weaknesses:

- Recognizes own strengths
- Recognizes own developmental needs.

### How Do *You* Put It in Action?

#### Activity #1

To begin to self assess your capacity in **understanding your own strengths and weaknesses**, reflect on what it looks like when you perform each of the behaviors. List some specific examples from your own practice as evidence that you can and do perform this behavior.

| Personal Reflection: My View | |
| --- | --- |
| **Behavior/descriptor** | **Give examples of your performance of this behavior and the frequency with which it occurs. Be specific.** |
| Recognizes own strengths | |
| Recognizes own developmental needs | |

#### Activity #2

Discuss **understanding your own strengths and weaknesses** and its indicators with your supervisor, mentor, or coach. Elicit feedback regarding your effectiveness in demonstrating these skills. Discuss strategies for practice that builds greater capacity.

| Feedback: View of a Colleague, Supervisor, Mentor, or Coach | | |
| --- | --- | --- |
| **Behavior/descriptor** | **Effectiveness in demonstrating** | **Strategies to build capacity** |
| Recognizes own strengths | | |
| Recognizes own developmental needs | | |

## Activity #3

Complete the following chart to assess your ability in this skill. You will use the results to develop your personal learning plan in Chapter 7.

| Understanding Your Own Strengths and Weaknesses: How Do *You* Put It in Action? | |
|---|---|
| **Gather & Analyze Data** | **Ask:** How is my on-the-job performance in this skill area?<br><br>■ Reflect on your performance of the understanding your own strengths and weaknesses behavioral indicators—the frequency with which you engage in each behavior as opposed to your ability to perform the behavior.<br><br>■ Solicit face-to-face feedback from a variety of sources—such as a mentor, a coach, a supervisor, supervisees, and colleagues—that focuses on the understanding your own strengths and weaknesses indicators.<br><br>■ Seek anonymous feedback from the 360-degree tool available from NASSP (www.principals.org).<br><br>■ Seek data from a formal assessment process (e.g., Selecting and Developing 21st Century Leaders and Leadership Skills Assessments from NASSP).<br><br>■ Review your performance on the indicators. Discuss the results with mentor or colleague. |
| **Possible Solutions & Strategies** | Assignments that stretch and provide practice in this skill:<br><br>■ Focus your professional reading for a period of time on professional publications that feature articles and stories about innovations. Reflect on projects that address areas of concern in your school or district and appear to be "innovative," i.e., an approach not previously used in your school or district. Structure opportunities to interact with creative teachers and administrators and share ideas about things that could and should be done in the school or your district.<br><br>■ Practice communicating your personal educational values and vision to others in both written and oral forms. Seek feedback regarding the communication of educational values and vision in correspondence and other written material.<br><br>■ Seek opportunities to chair problem-solving committees at the school or district level. Ask a mentor or colleague to monitor progress and provide feedback regarding effective use of planning skills and follow-through.<br><br>■ Attend to your mental and physical health. Plan to do something that you enjoy and that provides physical exercise.<br><br>■ Establish a monthly pattern of reading one or two books or articles in professional areas other than education.<br><br>■ Make a chart of your educational/professional goals. **Ask**, "Where do I want to be and when?" Develop an action plan to accomplish your goals. Periodically review your goals statements and action plans, and reflect on your progress. Revise as necessary.<br><br>■ Work with a mentor or colleague, family members, and possibly your doctor to assess the work, family, social, physical, and emotional demands on you. Develop strategies and action plans to maintain balance between your personal needs and the complex demands on a school administrator. |

| **Possible Solutions & Strategies** | **Workshops, seminars, and courses** |
|---|---|

_____

_____

_____

■ Check your district, regional service agency, state department, or colleges and universities in your area for opportunities for building capacity in this skill area.

**Mentor, coaches, and supervisors**

_____

_____

_____

**Ask:** Who can mentor me in this area and help me prioritize issues?

What are the questions I can ask a mentor about behavior and practice in this area?

■ Develop a mentor relationship with a trusted colleague who is highly motivated. Review personal career goals with the mentor. Discuss the development or the refinement of short-range and long-range career goals and an accompanying career development plan.

■ Discuss with a mentor or colleague techniques used to effectively cope with stress.

**Readings** (see Appendix 5 for an extensive list)

Bennis, W., & Goldsmith, J. (2003). *Learning to lead: A workbook on becoming a leader.* New York, NY: Basic Books.

Covey, S. R., Merrill, R. A., & Merrill, R. R. (1996). *First things first.* New York, NY: Free Press.

Kaplan, R. E. & Drath, W. H. (1991). *Beyond ambition: How driven managers can lead better and live better.* San Francisco, CA: Jossey-Bass.

**Off-the-job development opportunities**

_____

_____

_____

**Ask:** What organizations and committees can I become active in to practice the behaviors?

■ Become more actively involved in the work of the professional associations of which you are a member.

**NASSP professional development opportunities**

■ Online courses

■ Seminars

■ Web-based resources

■ Customized professional development

(Visit www.principals.org/ProfessionalDevelopment.aspx to see current offerings.)

| | |
|---|---|
| **Assess Readiness & Build Capacity** | **Ask:** What do climate surveys, such as CASE from NASSP, tell me about the readiness and the capacity of the school community (faculty members, students, and parents) that will affect how and whether I implement a solution?<br><br>_____<br>_____<br>_____<br><br>Who will be affected by my personal development activities in this skill area? How?<br><br>_____<br>_____<br>_____<br><br>What specific development in this skill area can I engage in that will have the greatest impact on my personal and professional capacity and the needs of the school?<br><br>_____<br>_____<br>_____<br><br>What school data (e.g., achievement; attendance, graduation, and drop-out rates; demographics; and instructional staff qualifications, experience, and background) affect my professional development needs and the possible solutions I identified? How?<br><br>_____<br>_____<br>_____ |
| **Create & Communicate Plan** | See page 109 to develop your plan.<br>**Ask:** How will I share my personal learning plan with others?<br><br>_____<br>_____<br>_____<br><br>Specifically, how will I encourage every adult in my school to have a learning plan based on their developmental needs in the context of the needs of the school and the students?<br><br>_____<br>_____<br>_____ |
| **Implement Plan** | This is how I will practice the indicators to build capacity in the skill:<br><br>_____<br>_____<br>_____ |

| **Monitor & Adjust** | These are the specific measures of progress I will use in this skill area: |
|---|---|
| | _____ |
| | _____ |
| | _____ |
| | These are the specific measures of progress I will use to determine the impact my progress in this area is having on the needs of the school: |
| | _____ |
| | _____ |
| | _____ |
| | This is the feedback I will solicit: (when, from whom, in what form): |
| | _____ |
| | _____ |
| | _____ |
| | I will use these aids to help in my development (e.g., reflection, journaling): |
| | _____ |
| | _____ |
| | _____ |
| | Return to "Gather & Analyze Data" at the beginning of this instrument to establish new priorities within the same skill or to begin work on another skill. |

## How Your Colleagues Put It in Action

Below you will find excerpts from interviews of several middle level and high school leaders related to **understanding your own strengths and weaknesses**.

"You have to realize that you're the lead learner at the school. You don't know everything, so it's important that you keep abreast of the literature, new methods, and technologies. The teacher is going to look to the principal for direction and guidance.

"Every professional development activity that takes place in our school, I attend. The worst thing that I could do would be to have a professional development strategy or a session here at school and then not show up. Because the teachers are going to say, 'If it's not important for him, why do I have to be here?'

"We do a lot of professional development work through book studies. Our system also supports our need to attend local, regional, and national conferences. We've been lucky enough to do several presentations at national conferences, and while we are there we take advantage of the other sessions going on. I like to say that I've never had an original idea in my life, but I sure stumbled on a lot of ideas from a lot of good folks around the country."

—Ray Landers, Principal, Boaz (AL) Middle School,
MetLife/NASSP 2009 National Middle Level Principal of the Year

"We ask a lot of our teachers. People have a need to be a part of something bigger than themselves. I think it's one of the reasons that people have a sense of community, and I think it's one of the reasons that people thrive in certain organizations. Opportunity is one of the greatest things anybody can ever give to you. If we were cookie-cutter about the way we operated, I don't think we'd be feeding our teachers. I think we feed them with opportunity. I also think we feed them with professional learning: that whole dynamic where teachers are dependent upon each other, they're talking to each other, they're growing and learning from each other as experts—all of that goes into feeding our teachers. We also feed them with respect.

"We respect what's going on in that classroom. And because of that respect, because we believe that what we're doing is so important. I really believe that people who work here feel like they're a part of something bigger than themselves, they feel like they're a part of something that's driven by success, they feel like they're part of something that's high expectations. And because of that, they like coming here."

—Mark Wilson, Principal, Morgan County High School, Madison, GA, MetLife/NASSP 2009 National High School Principal of the Year

---

"I'm always learning. Claughton Middle School by no means has all the answers in the world, so being open to seeing what's working in schools all across America will help you find the answers. Any kind of networking or sharing or just watching can only make you better as a person. It's just wonderful to see that there are schools across the nation that are succeeding with students at high levels, and [it's] refreshing to know that there are many, many ideas out there. So the solutions to student academic achievement are out there."

—Delic Loyde, Principal, Stelle Claughton Middle School, Houston, TX, a 2009 MetLife-NASSP Breakthrough School

---

"I remember the assessment center…it was the spring of my first year as principal so I was past the honeymoon period, and I may have been questioning how I was doing at the school. The thing I remember most was that these people who were assessing me, sitting across the table from me, were telling me that I was doing lots of things well. Sure there were things that I could do better, and some things I needed to think about, but that I was going to be okay and would be a good principal and get even better. In times of doubt, I would tend to go back and review "my folder," and remind myself that I have signature strengths that others observed in practice.

"Before I started in a school, I was uncomfortable giving feedback, so I visited with someone who was very good at it and observed. I also participated in NASSP's Springfield program. A benefit of structure is that I was forced to give feedback over time— to practice a skill that I needed to work on—and people were there to guide me as to whether the feedback I was giving was good or helpful. Just helping me figure out how to plan a conversation has been very helpful. Here's how you do it, now let's practice it by creating a difficult scenario…and here are the skill to address.

"For example, planning a conversation around an issue that school leaders must address such as a student or teacher not performing, you need to practice for that conversation: here is the behavior we want eliminated, here is how it impacts the school, how are we going to address this? There are a number of skills involved including sensitivity. You are stating the facts, eliciting feedback, and practicing judgment and results orientation.

"For somebody who says they are too busy to reflect through a process they might be working too hard rather than smart. One principal I worked with said that he discovered through his assessment that he was doing things that the staff should have been doing as part of a collaborative leadership process. The next day he went into school and immediately changed some things and shared responsibilities. He was much happier and less stressed after that.

"Nobody can understand the principal's job at any specific school until they are the principal. When I was an assistant principal, I thought I knew, but then I became a principal—and it was a lonely job—and a lot of new principals struggle with that. They need to be collaborative much more with faculty and be part of teams.

"My experience tells me that there are many districts that say they have leadership development programs or other programs for aspiring leaders. Too often those programs simply bring in speakers, watch a movie, or build knowledge rather than skills."

—Morgan Lee, Education Associate, South Carolina Department of Education, Columbia

### Activity #4

To practice identifying the behavioral indicators related to **understanding your own strengths and weaknesses**, list the indicators that you saw in the actions of these school leaders.

| Behavioral Indicators Identified | Practice, Action, or Sentiment From Interviews |
|---|---|
|  |  |
|  |  |
|  |  |
|  |  |

### Reference

Fuller, E. (2007). *Principal turnover, teacher turnover and quality and student achievement* [PowerPoint]. Presentation at the meeting of the National Policy Board for Educational Administrators, December 12, 2007, University of Texas, Austin. Retrieved from NPBEA Web site: www.npbea.org/meetings/NPBEA_12.9.07.ppt

# 7 Putting It All Together: Your Personal Learning Plan

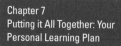

*Genius is 99 percent perspiration and 1 percent inspiration.*

—*Thomas Edison*

How often are great masters of art or inventors of game-changing innovations and technologies described as being formulaic? Not often. Although they relied on knowledge and processes that already existed, they aspired to build upon the genius of previous generations, not to simply learn what was already known. The quest to attain higher or more robust goals—or new ways of doing things—requires inspiration. Students dream about new frontiers. Teachers extol the virtues of creativity and uniqueness and help students reach for the stars. Principals encourage and support teachers to bring out the best in students, to challenge students to dream and succeed.

As a leader within your school and community, you must foster that inspiration in staff members and students. Throughout this guide are tools to help you understand how you can become a better instructional and administrative leader by assessing your strengths and weaknesses. Now is the time to pull all those pieces together into a plan that will enable you to practice and develop behaviors to increase your skill bank. Although your leadership must be inspirational to others, leadership is hard work. It doesn't just come naturally.

A personal learning plan is one way to tie all the assessments and analyses together and show how interconnected the skills are. The work you have done in the previous chapters should make the completion of your personal learning plan much easier—and more beneficial.

## Creating the Plan

It is time to start planning. You have gathered information about yourself from your work in the previous chapters and from your consideration of a variety of developmental strategies. Think about the skill dimensions that have emerged as high priority areas of development for you. Your developmental priorities should be based on your own strengths or weaknesses as well as the needs of your school. Ask yourself, what do I need to develop in myself to be a better leader while meeting the needs of my school? For example, if setting instructional direction is a weakness for you, then improving instruction in your school will only happen if you strengthen that set of skills.

Review your work in the previous chapters. Make a decision about which skill will be your initial developmental focus. Starting with one skill will focus your efforts on building your capacity in that skill as you engage in improving your school. In other words, you can't address the needs of the school without developing your skill to do so.

You have made a decision. Now, use the spaces below to list a skill dimension and the behavioral indicators you want to develop.

| **Skill Dimension:** | |
|---|---|
| Specific behavioral indicators: | |
| | |

Refer to the lists of suggested developmental strategies from previous chapters and from Appendix 6. Select and list the strategies you plan to carry out. Include multiple categories from among assignments, workshops and seminars, work with a mentor, readings, off-the-job activities, and NASSP offerings to increase your potential for successful professional growth.

| | |
|---|---|
| 1. | |
| 2. | |
| 3. | |
| 4. | |
| 5. | |
| 6. | |
| 7. | |
| 8. | |
| 9. | |
| 10. | |

## Action Plan

Create an action plan to accomplish the strategies listed above. Identify opportunities within your present job responsibilities or seek out special activities and projects that will allow you to focus on your development objectives.

Consider the ways you can:

- Tap the expertise of experienced administrators in education and other fields
- Locate relevant reference material
- Participate in professional courses, seminars, and workshops
- Affiliate with professional organizations
- Serve in field assignments such as internships
- Fill in for an administrator who is on leave
- Organize special projects within the school, district, or community.

Ask yourself:

- What will I do to build my capacity?
- Who will be involved or affected?
- When and where will it be done?
- How will it be monitored and who will provide feedback regarding your progress or performance?
- How does it relate to the school improvement plan?

Be as specific as possible when answering these questions. The more detailed your plan is, the easier it will be to follow the plan and to accomplish your goals for professional growth.

## Keeping a Journal or Behavioral Log

Your development ultimately boils down to what you do with your opportunities and abilities. There is no guaranteed path to success. There is virtually no correlation between years of experience and effectiveness as a leader. What really matters is how you learn from your experiences. All assignments have developmental elements. After all, it is not the assignment that matters as much as what it requires you to do and how you learn from it. Learning from experiences requires the ability to look inside yourself and deal with your own feelings and motives. To be effective, experience must be related to your strengths, shortcomings, and defenses.

Successful leaders know themselves. Self-knowledge comes from seeking feedback from others, reflecting on what you are doing, being honest with yourself, and not letting success go to your head. The important factors in your development plan will be your ability to learn from your experiences and observations. Keeping a journal facilitates this process by aiding you in maintaining your developmental focus and fostering effective reflection on your experiences.

Use the journal to record what is happening to you and how it affects your skill development. As you develop your leadership skills, it is important to reflect on your learning experiences and to record your thoughts. The journal ties all your learning experiences together. Writing in your journal—putting your feelings and perceptions into words—will further enhance your learning experience. The journal will also help you share your experiences with a mentor or colleague.

Use the following journal format or adapt it to work for you. Develop a strategy to ensure that you engage in reflection: Set aside 15 minutes at the end of each day to reflect on your development plan as it relates to the events of the day. Ask yourself if you learned anything from an assignment, a supervisor, a challenge, a development activity, or an off-the-job experience. Ask yourself, what did I do well or not-so-well? What will I do the same or differently next time? Capture those ideas in your journal.

## Journal/Behavior Log

NAME:

| DATE/TIME | SITUATION | SKILL | REFLECTION |
|-----------|-----------|-------|------------|
|           |           |       |            |
|           |           |       |            |
|           |           |       |            |
|           |           |       |            |
|           |           |       |            |

# APPENDIX 1
# 21st Century Principal Skills and Their Relationship to Standards

## 21st Century Principal Skills: Definitions

| | |
|---|---|
| **Setting Instructional Direction (SID)** | Implementing strategies for improving teaching and learning including putting programs and improvement efforts into action. Developing a vision of learning and establishing clear goals; providing direction in achieving stated goals; encouraging others to contribute to goal achievement; securing commitment to a course of action from individuals and groups. |
| **Teamwork (T)** | Seeking and encouraging involvement of team members. Modeling and encouraging the behaviors that move the group to task completion. Supporting group accomplishment. |
| **Sensitivity (S)** | Perceiving the needs and concerns of others; dealing tactfully with others in emotionally stressful situations or in conflict. Knowing what information to communicate and to whom. Relating to people of varying ethnic, cultural, and religious backgrounds. |
| **Judgment (J)** | Ability to make high quality decisions based on data; skill in identifying educational needs and setting priorities; assigning appropriate priority to issues; and in exercising caution. Ability to seek, analyze, and interpret relevant data. |
| **Results Orientation (RO)** | Assuming responsibility. Recognizing when a decision is required. Taking prompt action based on data as issues emerge. Resolving short-term issues while balancing them against long-term objectives. |
| **Organization Ability (OA)** | Planning and scheduling one's own and the work of others so that resources are used appropriately. Scheduling flow of activities; establishing procedures to monitor projects. Practicing time and task management; knowing what to delegate and to whom. |
| **Oral Communication (OC)** | Clearly communicating. Making oral presentations that are clear and easy to understand. |
| **Written Communication (WC)** | Ability to express ideas clearly and correctly in writing; to write appropriately for different audiences—students, teachers, parents, and others. |
| **Developing Others (DO)** | Teaching, coaching, and helping others. Providing specific feedback based on observations and data. |
| **Understanding Own Strengths and Weaknesses (USW)** | Identifying personal strengths and weaknesses. Taking responsibility for improvement by actively pursuing developmental activities. Striving for continuous learning. |

## Standards and Skills for School Leaders in the 21st Century

National, state, and local entities have developed various sets of standards for school leaders. Many of these standards include knowledge, disposition, and/or performance outcomes. To meet standards, school leaders must perform. Performance is grounded in skills as evidenced by behavior. The 21st Century School Administrator Skills are some of the skills that make possible the performances described in standards. The appropriate knowledge imbedded in the skills set forms a foundation upon which to build school leadership mastery.

The Interstate School Leaders Licensure Consortium (ISLLC) Standards for School Leaders, recently revised and renamed the Educational Leadership Policy Standards: ISLLC 2008, have been developed by a consortium sponsored by the National Policy Board for Educational Administration.

The relationship between the Educational Leadership Policy Standards: ISLLC 2008 and the 21st Century School Administrator Skills is similar to that which exists between any set of standards and requisite skill sets. The standards spell out the performance desired of highly effective leaders in specific categories or areas. Effective performance requires the complex integration of a wide variety of behaviors composed of thoughts, words, and actions. The behaviors are based on skills.

The 21st Century School Administrator Skills were derived from an extensive job analysis of the principalship. These skills enable school leaders to meet performance standards. For example, the first standard from the Educational Leadership Policy Standards: ISLLC 2008 is "An education leader promotes the success of every student by facilitating the development, articulation, implementation, and stewardship of a vision of learning that is shared and supported by all stakeholders."

What skills are associated with successfully meeting this standard?

An examination of the words in the standard gives clues to the skills required for meeting it: skills to promote the success of all students, to develop a shared vision of learning, to articulate that vision orally and in writing, to implement goals and objectives congruent with the vision, and to nurture and care for the vision of learning so that it is shared and supported by the school community. Skills that are essential to success in these tasks are setting instructional direction, teamwork, sensitivity, results orientation, organizational ability, oral and written communication, and developing others. Elements of other skills also may be needed. Use the matrix [Figure A1] to specify the essential skills that you think are essential to meeting each of the Educational Leadership Policy Standards: ISLLC 2008. Use the skill definitions to assist you as you explore the skills and the Educational Leadership Policy Standards: ISLLC 2008 and their relationship to one another.

## Activity
### Understanding the 21st Century Skill Dimensions—Relating the Skills to the Educational Leadership Policy Standards: ISLLC 2008

The purpose of this activity is to deepen your understanding of the standards and skills in the context of a school setting. Although all of the skills are required for each standard, limiting the number specified for each standard forces deeper processing of the standard and the skills.

Use the 21st Century Skills Definitions and behavioral indicators and the matrix on the following page to specify the three or four skills that you think are requisite to meeting each of the ISLLC standards. Refer to the skill definitions to assist in your exploration of the skills and the ISLLC standards and their relationship to one another. Place a check in the box under the skill dimension abbreviation. Repeat the process for each standard.

Compare and discuss your choices with a colleague or mentor. Be prepared to support your decisions with examples from your experience in school leadership.

Share the activity with colleagues. Discuss your insights and perspectives of the standards, skills, and their relationships. Discuss how you might enhance your performance by focusing on skill development.

**Mentors:** Consider how you might use this activity to assist a protégé in building leadership capacity.

Figure A1

# Educational Leadership Policy Standards: ISLLC 2008

| Standard 1 | SID | T | S | J | RO | OA | OC | WC | DO | USW |
|---|---|---|---|---|---|---|---|---|---|---|
| An education leader promotes the success of every student by facilitating the development, articulation, implementation, and stewardship of a vision of learning that is shared and supported by all stakeholders. | | | | | | | | | | |

| Standard 2 | SID | T | S | J | RO | OA | OC | WC | DO | USW |
|---|---|---|---|---|---|---|---|---|---|---|
| An education leader promotes the success of every student by advocating, nurturing, and sustaining a school culture and instructional program conducive to student learning and staff professional growth. | | | | | | | | | | |

| Standard 3 | SID | T | S | J | RO | OA | OC | WC | DO | USW |
|---|---|---|---|---|---|---|---|---|---|---|
| An education leader promotes the success of every student by ensuring management of the organization, operations, and resources for a safe, efficient, and effective learning environment. | | | | | | | | | | |

| Standard 4 | SID | T | S | J | RO | OA | OC | WC | DO | USW |
|---|---|---|---|---|---|---|---|---|---|---|
| An education leader who promotes the success of every student by collaborating with faculty and community members, responding to diverse community interests and needs, and mobilizing community resources. | | | | | | | | | | |

| Standard 5 | SID | T | S | J | RO | OA | OC | WC | DO | USW |
|---|---|---|---|---|---|---|---|---|---|---|
| An education leader promotes the success of every student by acting with integrity, fairness, and in an ethical manner. | | | | | | | | | | |

| Standard 6 | SID | T | S | J | RO | OA | OC | WC | DO | USW |
|---|---|---|---|---|---|---|---|---|---|---|
| An education leader who promotes the success of every student by understanding, responding to, and influencing the larger political, social, economic, legal, and cultural context. | | | | | | | | | | |

# APPENDIX 2
# Advanced Standards for School Leaders

S imilar to the national board certification for teachers, the National Board for Professional Teaching Standards (NBPTS) is in the process of developing certification for school principals that will rely on adherence to core propositions. The NASSP skills and behaviors explicated in this guide help equip leaders to accomplish the complex performances detailed in the following core propositions for educational leaders.

## Core Propositions for Educational Leaders

1. Accomplished educational leaders continuously cultivate their understanding of leadership and the change process to meet high levels of performance. (Leadership)
2. Accomplished educational leaders model professional, ethical behavior and expect it from others. (Ethics)
3. Accomplished educational leaders have a clear vision and inspire and engage stakeholders in developing and realizing the mission. (Vision)
4. Accomplished educational leaders are committed to student and adult learners and to their development. (Learners and Learning)
5. Accomplished educational leaders drive, facilitate, and monitor the teaching and learning process. (Instruction)
6. Accomplished educational leaders act with a sense of urgency to foster a cohesive culture of learning. (Culture)
7. Accomplished educational leaders manage and leverage systems and processes to achieve desired results. (Management)
8. Accomplished educational leaders ensure equitable learning opportunities and high expectations for all. (Equity)
9. Accomplished educational leaders advocate on behalf of their schools, communities, and profession. (Advocacy)

A more complete rationale for the certification is provided below in remarks by the NBPTS president Joseph A. Aguerrebere Jr. made at the 2009 MetLife/NASSP National Principal of the Year awards in Washington, DC:

The National Board for Professional Teaching Standards, at the urging of others, has begun the development of national board certification for school principals. Just like our board certification process for teachers, which is now considered the gold standard for accomplished teaching, we are working to create a rigorous and meaningful assessment process that identifies what principals should know and are able to do. This assessment would not be for entry level licensure, but rather to identify and recognize practice at an accomplished level. Just like board certification which is a career stage well accepted in other professions like medicine, or accounting or architecture, educators also will be able to reach for a higher bar, achieve it, and be recognized for it....

The first step was to come to professional consensus around a set of value statements that we call core propositions that reflect the leadership dimensions that accurately capture what it means to be an educational leader in schools today and into the future. They provide a broad conceptual framework upon which we can identify specific standards for principals. This involved intensive but productive meetings where representatives from around the country worked...to prepare a draft document that was presented for public review and comment through an online process. About 5000 individuals from around the country commented on all or part of the document. Every comment was reviewed and considered in the final version. This summer a working group worked intensively to build a set of standards for school principals. Another 2,800 individuals commented on the draft standards. These standards are intended to capture the knowledge, skills, and dispositions necessary to be considered accomplished.

The standards are part of a patchwork quilt of factors that contribute to success. Pulling on the thread of part of the quilt will likely affect another part. The National Board's image of an accomplished principal will recognize that there are simultaneously science, art, and craft dimensions to the practice of leadership of a school. An effective principal understands that certain practices yield better results than other practices, depending on the context and circumstances. This underscores the notion that leading a school is part science, in that there is a growing body of research identifying particular practices and behaviors that are more effective. The research in the fields of organizational behavior and organizational psychology across a range of sectors can help us understand better about the science of leadership.

The artistic dimension of leading a school acknowledges that there can be different paths to the same outcome. Two principals may lead and be equally effective in their schools, but have widely different styles based on their personalities, their interactive styles, and the culture and environment in which they are working. Effective principals use creativity, entrepreneurship, and style in accomplishing similar objectives. An effective principal understands that students and adults learn in different ways and require different approaches to reaching them.

Leading a school is also part craft that calls for developing professional judgment. Skilled principals reflect on their practice for the purpose of evaluating what worked and did not work so that adjustments can be made to be more effective. An effective principal understands that every context is different and requires judgments that are aligned with the vision and mission of the school. Like in any craft, professional judgment and practice is refined and improved over time. Some have called this the wisdom of practice. We understand the logic of this when we think of airplane pilots. Airplane pilots all undergo the same training for each type of plane they fly. They use simulations to assist in the training. But no one actually believes that a newly minted pilot is equal in skill and judgment to a similarly trained pilot who has logged thousands of flight hours under a variety of weather conditions and circumstances. This logic is true across the professions and should be no less true with a skilled principal who continues to stay current and motivated.

The assessment experience that we envision will provide a way to internalize and operationalize the standards and values that support accomplished practice. This valuable feedback could be used in many productive ways.

Though the assessment has not been developed yet, if we follow the approach that we used with teachers, the principal assessment will have certain characteristics. It will be comprehensive and rigorous. It will be tied to a set of standards that have been developed by peers and scholars in the field. It will be linked tightly to performance and results. It will ask for evidence of meeting each of the standards in ways that demonstrate performance and results. It will be an assessment that is taken over an extended period of time in order to gauge results. It will be real, authentic and relevant to the job asking for a portfolio of evidence. It will be an assessment that will force principals to answer tough questions about their practice.

If we get it right, principals will actually improve their practice and get better at what they do as a result of going through the process. So not only will we be able to identify accomplished practice but we will also provide a professional growth experience that will be second to none in the field. If we follow the practice of other professions, the assessments will be evaluated and scored by your peers in the field who do what you do. They will be trained to make valid and reliable judgments that can provide valuable information about your practice.

We will communicate to the larger public that we are a profession that holds itself to high standards and is willing to hold itself accountable. That we have a reliable and objective way to measure performance that can be used to recognize and reward excellence. We will also demonstrate that we can have a set of standards that are accepted and appropriate no matter where one works in this country. This will go a long way toward moving us away from having 50 different sets of state standards across the country. That means moving from a profession that is currently fragmented due to the variations across states and localities to a profession that is unified. When national board certification is recognized as the gold standard of effective practice, then this will contribute to having a designation that is more portable than the current state licensure structure. This could allow talent to move where it is needed the most without having to jump over bureaucratic hurdles. This hopefully will go a long way toward strengthening the profession as high professional standards and assessments have done in other professions that are held in high esteem.

Appendix 2
Advanced Standards for
School Leaders

# APPENDIX 3
# 21st Century Principal Skills: Behavioral Indicators

## Setting Instructional Direction

- Articulates a vision related to teaching and learning
- Articulates high performance expectations for self or others
- Encourages improvement in teaching and learning
- Sets clear measurable objectives
- Generates enthusiasm toward common goals
- Seeks to develop alliances outside the school to support high quality teaching and learning
- Acknowledges achievement or accomplishments
- Seeks commitment to a course of action

## Teamwork

- Supports the ideas of team members
- Encourages team members to share ideas
- Contributes ideas toward accomplishing the team's goals
- Assists in performing the operational tasks of the team
- Seeks input from team members
- Acts to maintain direction or focus to achieve the team's goals
- Seeks consensus among team members

## Sensitivity

- Interacts professionally and tactfully with others
- Elicits perceptions, feelings, or concerns of others
- Voices disagreement without creating unnecessary conflict
- Communicates necessary information to appropriate persons in a timely manner
- Expresses written, verbal, and/or nonverbal recognition of feelings, needs, or concerns in responding to others

## Judgment

- Takes action within the bounds of appropriate priority
- Acts with caution in approaching an unfamiliar person or situation
- Analyzes information to determine the important elements of a situation
- Communicates a clear rationale for a decision
- Seeks additional information
- Uses information sources that are relevant to an issue
- Asks follow-up questions to clarify information
- Seeks to identify the cause of a problem
- See relationships among issues

## Results Orientation

- Takes action to move issues toward closure
- Initiates action for improvement
- Determines the criteria that indicate a problem or issue is resolved
- Considers the implications of a decision before taking action
- Makes decisions on the basis of information
- Relates individual issues to the larger picture

## Organizational Ability

- Delegates responsibilities to others
- Plans to monitor delegated responsibilities
- Develops action plans
- Monitors progress
- Establishes timelines, schedules, or milestones
- Prepares for meetings
- Uses available resources

## Oral Communication

- Demonstrates effective presentation skills
- Speaks articulately
- Uses proper grammar, pronunciation, diction, and syntax
- Tailors messages to meet the needs of unique audiences
- Clearly presents thoughts and ideas in one-on-one, small group, and formal presentation settings

## Written Communication

- Writes concisely
- Demonstrates technical proficiency in writing
- Expresses ideas clearly in writing
- Writes appropriately for different audiences

## Developing Others

- Shares expertise gained through experience
- Encourages others to change behaviors that inhibit professional growth
- Recommends specific developmental strategies
- Asks others for their perceptions of their professional development needs
- Seeks agreement on specific actions to be taken for developmental growth

## Understanding Your Own Strengths and Weaknesses

- Recognizes own strengths
- Recognizes own developmental needs

Appendix 3
21st Century Principal Skills:
Behavioral Indicators

# APPENDIX 4
# Five Strategies for Using In-Basket Items

## Strategy 1: Analyzing Skills in Responses Written by Others

This activity uses prewritten responses to give you an opportunity to learn and practice the process of in-basket response analysis by analyzing data that is generated by someone else. Following this activity, you will write responses to in-basket items and engage in self, peer, or group-analysis of your responses. Select and read one in-basket item and the responses to the item.

- Reflect on the effective aspects of the response. Write briefly about the things that you think contribute to the response's effectiveness and explain your rationale.

- Reflect on the aspects of the response that are not effective. Write briefly about the things that you think contribute to the response's ineffectiveness and explain your rationale.

- Consider the overall effectiveness of the response. Is it a good or bad response? Justify your answer by focusing on the behaviors demonstrated by the writer. Which of the 10 skill dimensions are demonstrated (positively and negatively) in the response? Use the skill behavioral indicators list to guide your analysis. Which skills are not demonstrated that might contribute to a better response and outcome?

---

**Enrich your development experience.** Have a conversation with your mentor about your analysis of the responses. Ask a colleague to participate in the activity with you and have a conversation about your findings. Keep the conversation focused on the skills and behavioral indicators.

---

## Practice In-Basket Item A

> **From:** **Greg Jones, Language Arts Teacher**
> **Sent:** 01/23, 9:30 a.m.
> **Subject:** **Achievement problems**
>
> I've had it! Have you looked at the most recent reading comprehension scores for this school? It is a disgrace! I simply can't teach a class where nearly one-fourth of the students are achieving below grade level and are not motivated to learn. The students are rude and not interested in the positive aspects of school. I don't know where their values are. It seems to me that this is one of the most important problems facing our school.
>
> Something must be done to help these kids. I'd even be willing to work on a committee to look for solutions to this problem.
>
> My point is that all our efforts are to no avail if we must constantly re-teach these kids.

## Responses to In-Basket Item A

> ### From the Principal's Mailbox
>
> **Greg Jones, Language Arts Teacher**
> **Sent:** 01/25, 12:30 p.m.
> **Subject:** **RE: achievement problems**
>
> Greg,
> Try not to be so upset. I will look into this issue. I'll get back to you within the week. We will get this thing squared away.
>
> Please be patient.
>
> Thanks.

## From the Principal's Mailbox

**To:**       **Jo Martin, Assistant Principal**

**Sent:**     **01/25, 12:35 p.m.**

**Subject:**   **e-mail from Greg Jones**

Jo,

I received a pretty angry e-mail from Greg Jones complaining about student achievement (or lack thereof) in reading. He also mentioned rude students who were not motivated to learn. Can you give me any details on how he has been performing lately? He seems interested in helping to address this problem, but I need to know if he is doing okay with his teaching assignments before engaging him in an effort to improve reading achievement.

By midweek next could you give me some info on our recent and past reading scores?

I would also like your thoughts on what we do to confront the issue.

Thanks.

**Use the following questions to guide your analysis:**

- Are there opportunities to demonstrate skill in instructional leadership in responding to this item? Do you see any of these skills demonstrated in the responses above?
- Setting instructional direction? If so, which specific indicators?
- Teamwork? If so, which specific indicators?
- Sensitivity? If so, which specific indicators?
- Are there opportunities to demonstrate skill in resolving complex problems in responding to
  this item? Do you see any of these skills demonstrated in the responses above?
- Judgment? If so, which specific indicators?
- Results orientation? If so, which specific indicators?
- Organizational ability? If so, which specific indicators?
- Are there opportunities to demonstrate skill in developing others in responding to this item? If so, which specific indicators?

## Practice In-Basket Item B

**From:** Leslie Daniels, Chairperson, Assessment Committee
**Sent:** 10/15, 9:37 p.m.
**Subject:** Elimination of School Assessment Committee

I just wrapped up a meeting of five of the seven members of last year's School Assessment Committee here in my home. We met here because we fear that we no longer have any standing as far as the school district is concerned.

We understand that the school board is about to make a very rash decision and unanimously agree that we must register our opposition to the arbitrary manner in which the Board of Education plans to eliminate our committee. We feel strongly that such action by the Board will drain the community of any real influence. We have heard that the local school committees will replace the assessment committee. It seems to us that this suggests an entirely new emphasis and direction. The assessment committee was originally charged with evaluating the school program, and now my understanding is that the local school committee will have only a surveying and advisory function. Assessing implies some type of evaluation, while surveying indicates only the collection of data and reporting the status quo.

We are writing you in hopes that you will use your influence to help prevent this change in policy and to maintain the composition and function of the assessment committee as it was originally intended.

We look forward to hearing from you or to speaking further with you regarding this matter.

## Responses to In-Basket Item B

### From the Principal's Mailbox

**To:** Leslie Daniels, Chairperson, Assessment Committee
**Sent:** 10/22, 9:35 a.m.
**Subject:** RE: Elimination of School Assessment Committee
**CC:** Dr. Witherspoon, Assoc. Supt. for Administration

I am sorry that you have had to wait for more than a week for a response to your e-mail. I first read the e-mail this morning and felt the need to respond to you immediately.

I will be glad to meet with you and your colleagues once I have gathered some information and a perspective on the issue. Please give me until the first week in November to get the information I will need. If you will please call me on Friday, November 6, I will arrange a meeting for the following week.

Please know that I will do whatever I can to work with you and your group in a productive manner. I look forward to meeting with you.

**To:** Dr. Witherspoon, Assoc. Supt. for Administration

**Sent:** 10/22, 9:45 a.m.

**Subject:** RE: Elimination of School Assessment Committee

I copied you on my response to Leslie Daniels' concerns about the elimination of the School Assessment Committee. This is the first news I've had of such a move. Please inform me as to the possibilities of such an action before I meet with Daniels and other committee members.

I do believe in maintaining strong involvement of parents and community members in our efforts to provide a strong educational program for all the students we serve. Where is the district moving in this regard?

I look forward to hearing from you.

## Use the following questions to guide your analysis:

- Are there opportunities to demonstrate skill in instructional leadership in responding to this item? Do you see any of these skills demonstrated in the responses above?
- Setting instructional direction? If so, which specific indicators?
- Teamwork? If so, which specific indicators?
- Sensitivity? If so, which specific indicators?
- Are there opportunities to demonstrate skill in resolving complex problems in responding to
  this item? Do you see any of these skills demonstrated in the responses above?
- Judgment? If so, which specific indicators?
- Results orientation? If so, which specific indicators?
- Organizational ability? If so, which specific indicators?
- Are there opportunities to demonstrate skill in developing others in responding to this item? If so, which specific indicators? Do you see any of these skills demonstrated in the responses above?

## Strategy 2: Writing and Analyzing Your Own Responses

Select several in-basket items at the appropriate instructional level from the ones included on the following pages. Respond in writing to the items as if you are the principal presented with the situations. Respond quickly with the information you have available. After you have responded to the items, reflect on your responses. Write brief descriptions of your rationale for each response. Use the following questions to guide analysis of your responses.

- What opportunities did the in-basket item present to demonstrate skill in **instructional leadership?** Which of these skills did you demonstrate in your response?

- **Setting instructional direction?** If so, which specific indicators?
- **Teamwork?** If so, which specific indicators?
- **Sensitivity?** If so, which specific indicators?

What opportunities did the in-basket item present to demonstrate skill in **resolving complex problems?** Which of these skills did you demonstrate in your response?

- **Judgment?** If so, which specific indicators?
- **Results orientation?** If so, which specific indicators?
- **Organizational ability?** If so, which specific indicators?
- Are there opportunities to demonstrate skill in **developing others** in responding to this item? If so, which specific indicators?

---

**Enrich your development experience.** Have a conversation with your mentor about your analysis of your responses. Seek your mentor's input into the analysis in terms of skills you demonstrate well, additional skills that might contribute to more a effective response, and skills that need practice.

Ask a colleague to participate in the activity with you. After your self-analysis, analyze each other's responses. Have a conversation about your findings. Keep the conversation focused on the skills and behavioral indicators. Discuss similarities and differences in your approaches to the task to explore personal organizational strategies.

---

## Strategy 3: Reinforcing Understanding of the Skills

Select in-basket items from among those provided below. Read each in-basket item. Using a copy of the 21st Century Principals Skills and Behavioral Indicators, (see Appendix 3) determine which skills should be used in handling each of the issues.

Record the skills and behaviors that should be used for several items and compare the similarities and differences in your responses. This strategy sheds light on the skills that you lead with in various situations. A person who leads with judgment skills might always look for more data, spend more time in analysis of information, or act with caution. A person who leads with sensitivity might always seek to take care of the human needs of everyone involved in the situation. Developing a self-awareness of the *habits* or skills with which one leads is important for understanding how a balance of individual strengths is essential to effective leadership.

---

**Enrich your development experience.** Have a conversation with your mentor about his perceptions of skills that should be used in responding to different in-basket issues. Seek your mentor's input into the analysis of the skills you selected and patterns that may indicate the behaviors with which you lead.

Ask a colleague to participate in the activity with you. Keep the conversation focused on the skills and behavioral indicators. Discuss what think would or should be done in response to each issue and the skills necessary to effectively accomplish that act. Reflect together on how patterns of behavior might contribute to understanding one's leading strengths and style.

---

## Strategy 4: Reflecting on Past Performance

Collect in-basket items and responses from your own work experience. Use strategy 1 with these items to reflect on and rate your responses. Use strategy 2 to construct new responses with an eye toward skills that might contribute to a better result. Use strategy 3 to look for what you did versus what you think might have been a better skills-focused approach.

> **Enrich your development experience.** If you decide to involve your mentor or colleagues in this activity, remember that confidentiality is an issue in examining situations that relate to real people and events. In some instances, names and other data should be changed to protect the privacy of third-party individuals.

## Strategy 5: Exploring the Underlying Issues

Using any of the previous strategies and in-basket materials, consider the issues presented by the in-basket item, such as supervision of staff, parent and community relationships, public health, or students with special needs. What do you know or need to know about these issues to build your knowledge base and enhance your performance as you combine knowledge and skills to enhance your leadership capacity?

> **Enrich your development experience.** Enrich your experience through conversations with colleagues and mentors about issues and resources.

## Sample In-Basket Items

The following items are appropriate for middle level and high schools and may easily be modified for elementary schools.

| | |
|---|---|
| **From:** | **Martha Evans, Secretary** |
| **Sent:** | **10/13, 10:30 a.m.** |
| **Subject:** | **Phone message** |

Mrs. Giflin called. She was very upset. Last week her son, Steve, and another boy were shoving each other in a friendly way as they went to their seats. Unfortunately, they knocked over a science experiment that Mr. Herrera had just set up for class.

Mr. Herrera lost his temper and used a racial slur, according to Mrs. Giflin. Steve has refused to do his science homework or to do anything in class except sit there. Mr. Herrera says he is going to fail Steven.

| | |
|---|---|
| **From:** | **Barbara Swan, Librarian/Media Specialist** |
| **Sent:** | **10/13, 10:35 a.m.** |
| **Subject:** | **Missing video** |

Last spring I requested, and you approved, a multimedia series on thinking skills.

Miss Howard has requested this for use next week, and I can't find it anywhere.

Did it ever arrive?

| | |
|---|---|
| **From:** | **Martha Evans, Secretary** |
| **Sent:** | **10/13, 10:37 a.m.** |
| **Subject:** | **Phone message** |

Mrs. Clarkson wants your help with Jud Robinson. She doesn't want to see him in class again.

She gave him an in-school suspension after all else failed. He is just completely disruptive in class. He is turned off and wants to drop out, but his father forces him to stay in school. Consequently, he's totally hostile and disruptive.

He didn't show up for the suspension, which started yesterday. He was hanging around the west entrance this morning, but he didn't come to class. We called his home and he is there.

## From the Principal's Mailbox

**From:** Liz Howard, Teacher
**Sent:** 10/13, 10:42 a.m.
**Subject:** Foul odor in restroom

There is a terrible smell in the first-floor boy's restroom by the west entrance. Smells like a sewer!!!

## From the Principal's Mailbox

**From:** Martha Evans, Secretary
**Sent:** 10/13, 10:45 a.m.
**Subject:** The Parents for Better Education (PBE) meeting

Mrs. Swanson, PBE President, has asked you to speak at the December meeting. If you can do this, I'll need to have your three main points right away in order to write something for their newsletter. Their deadline is October 20.

The topic is "What we need to do to have better education in America's middle level schools." Perhaps you could provide some explanation of some of the details of NCLB and its requirements for our school. What does it mean for a school to be designated as a school in need of improvement? What does AYP mean? These are terms we hear but probably don't understand fully as they relate to our school.

## From the Principal's Mailbox

**From:** Martha Evans, Secretary
**Sent:** 10/13, 11:00 a.m.
**Subject:** Message from the superintendent

The superintendent's secretary called. She wants you to put together something on cutting energy costs in school buildings for the next district principals meeting.

She needs to know right away if you can do it.

Appendix 4
Five Strategies for Using In-Basket Items

## From the Principal's Mailbox

**From:** Alice Howard, PTA President

**Sent:** 10/12, 11:05 a.m.

**Subject:** Fundraising success

The PTA just finished a very successful fundraising project that was a big success! We raised about $500 over our goal!

We'd like to use the money to sponsor a sock hop. We'll supply cold drinks and snacks—maybe even pizza!

We didn't want to tell the kids yet until you say it's OK. Or maybe you have another suggestion?

## From the Principal's Mailbox

**From:** Tom Evers, Social Studies Teacher

**Sent:** 10/13, 11:24 a.m.

**Subject:** Copier

It finally happened! The tired, old photocopier broke. Please, can we get something better? Something that leaves the background white and prints the words in black? Something that feeds and collates the pages? In other words, something that looks like it's from the 21st century. And SOON?

Also, may we use the office copier until the old machine is replaced? Seriously, we spend a lot of time at that machine and waste a lot of paper.

## From the Principal's Mailbox

**From:** Liz Howard, Math Teacher

**Sent:** 10/13, 11:25 a.m.

**Subject:** Health concern

Three days ago, I noticed that Janie Daniels had head lice. I immediately alerted the nurse, Sara Ferguson, but I haven't seen any notices going home. Has Sara taken action?

## From the Principal's Mailbox

**From:**     Elaine Fairfax, Grade 8 Team Leader
**Sent:**     10/13, 1:30 p.m.
**Subject:**  Phone message

Mrs. Haskell called to complain that her daughter has too much homework. She can't keep up with her classes. She wonders if someone isn't supposed to coordinate things.

I checked with Lee Soames, and she seems to think that language arts is the only class the kids have. She says that the teachers in the other teams don't require so many essays because they are lazy. I don't know about that, but I do know that one of the other teachers gives kids time in class to do the weekly essay.

What should I do? The complaint is about Lee Soames for giving too much homework, but I think that the others are giving too little.

## From the Principal's Mailbox

**From:**     Coach Glover
**Sent:**     10/13, 1:35 p.m.
**Subject:**  Dirty gym

The gym is dirty. It never gets swept up. Can you get the janitor to do it?

# APPENDIX 5
# Readings

Bennis, W. (2009). *On becoming a leader* (Rev. ed.). Philadelphia, PA: Basic Books.

Covey, S. R. (2004). *The seven habits of highly effective people: Powerful lessons in personal change.* New York, NY: Free Press.

Danielson, C. (2009). *Talk about teaching.* Thousand Oaks, CA: Corwin Press/NASSP.

Deal, T., & Peterson, K. (2009). *Shaping school culture: Pitfalls, paradoxes, & promises* (2nd. ed.). San Francisco, CA: Jossey-Bass.

Drucker, P. F. (2008). *The essential Drucker: The best of sixty years of Peter Drucker's essential writings on management.* New York, NY: Harperbusiness Essentials.

Drucker, P. F. (1995). *Managing in a time of great change.* New York, NY: Penguin Books.

Kouzes, J. M., & Posner, B. Z. (2007). *The leadership challenge* (4th ed.). San Francisco, CA: Jossey-Bass, Inc.

Hackman, J. R. (2002). *Leading teams.* Boston, MA: Harvard Business School Press.

Maddux, R. B., & Wingfield, B. (2003). *Team building: An exercise in leadership.* (4th ed.). Los Altos, CA: Crisp Publications.

Marzano, R. J., & Kendall, J. S. (2008). *Designing and assessing educational objectives: Applying the new taxonomy.* Thousand Oaks, CA: Corwin Press/NASSP.

Fullan, M. (2008). *Six secrets of change.* San Francisco, CA: Jossey-Bass

Salazar, P. (2008). *High-impact leadership for high impact schools: The actions that matter most.* Larchmont, NY: Eye on Education.

Senge, P., Kleiner, A., Roberts, C., Roth, G., Ross, R., & Smith, B. (1999). *The dance of change: The challenges to sustaining momentum in learning organizations.* New York, NY: Doubleday.

Katzenbach, J. R., & Smith, D. K. (2003). *The wisdom of teams: Creating the high performance organization.* Boston, MA: Harvard Business School Press.

Kouzes, J. M., Posner, B. Z., & Sheppard, R. (1999). *The leadership challenge planner: An action guide to achieving your personal best.* San Francisco, CA: Jossey-Bass.

Senge, P. M. (2006). *The fifth discipline: The art and practice of the learning organization.* New York, NY: Doubleday.

Whitaker, T. (2003). *Dealing with difficult teachers* (2nd ed.). Larchmont, NY: Eye on Education.

Reeves, D. B. (2009). *Leading change in your school: How to conquer myths, build commitment, and get results.* San Francisco, CA: Jossey-Bass.

Blanchard, K., & Johnson, S. (1982). *The one minute manager.* New York, NY: William Morrow.

Wiggins, G., & McTighe, J. (2004). *Understanding by design* (2nd ed.). Alexandria, VA: ASCD.

Colvin, G. (2007). Seven steps for developing a proactive schoolwide discipline plan: A guide for principals and leadership teams. Thousand Oaks, CA: Corwin Press.

Schmoker, M. J. (2006). *Results now: How we can achieve unprecedented improvements in teaching and learning.* Alexandria, VA: ASCD.

Marzano, R. (2003). *What works in schools.* Alexandria, VA: ASCD.

Hersey, P. (1997). *The situational leader.* Escondido, CA: Center for Leadership Studies

Stone, D. F., Patton, B., & Heen, S. (2000). *Difficult conversations: How to discuss what matters most.* New York, NY: Penguin.

Covey, S. R. (1989). Seven habits of highly effective people. New York, NY: Simon & Schuster.

Wagner, T., & Kegan, R. Change leadership: A practical guide to transforming our schools. San Francisco, CA: Jossey-Bass, 2006.

Parker, M., & Hoffman, R. (2006). Meeting excellence: 33 tools to lead meetings that get results. San Francisco, CA: Jossey-Bass.

Oncken, W. Jr., Burrows, H., & Blanchard, K. H. (1991). *The one minute manager meets the monkey.* New York, NY: William Morrow.

Smith, T. C. (1991). Making successful presentations: A self-teaching guide. New York, NY: Wiley.

Bates, J. D. (2000). *Writing with precision: How to write so that you cannot possibly be misunderstood.* New York, NY: Penguin.

# APPENDIX 6
# Developmental Strategies

The developmental strategies that follow will help you construct professional development plans. The suggestions are grouped by skill dimension; however, strategies listed in one area may apply to development of skill in other areas.

## Setting Instructional Direction

- Volunteer to serve on school or district committees to practice setting leadership direction in group situations.

- Seek feedback from an administrative mentor or a trusted colleague regarding personal leadership behavior strengths and areas for improvement that you have demonstrated in group situations.

- Study group dynamics in actual work groups and identify the behaviors that assist and those that hinder the groups in completing their tasks.

- Accept leadership of difficult ad hoc groups, inexperienced people, low-competence people, or loosely structured groups to practice bringing structure and direction to groups in order to accomplish tasks.

- Become active in community and professional organizations. Seek leadership roles within these organizations.

- Meet regularly with staff members to discuss their priorities. Provide input on the basis of your expectations as an instructional leader in the organization.

- When convening a committee to study a particular issue, use a written charge that you have drafted for that group. Include specifics relative to purpose or objectives for the group, the advisory or decision-making status of the group, resources that are available to assist in the group's work, to whom the group will report, your expectations, and deadlines or a timeline.

- Become an active participant in the school or district strategic-planning process. Instead of sending your team to the statewide training, conduct the training yourself. Include a module on change and the change process.

- With faculty members, attend training on new instructional methods and procedures to find new and better ways of doing things in the classroom.

- Organize your administrative team into focus groups. Create a cadre to train aspiring leaders within your own school or district and lead this group yourself.

- Focus your professional reading for a period of time on professional publications featuring articles and stories about innovations. Reflect on projects that address areas of concern in your school or district and appear innovative, i.e., an approach not previously used in your school or district.

- Structure opportunities to interact with creative teachers and administrators and share ideas about things that could and should be done in the school or your district.

- Participate in a district-level or state-level seminar or graduate course in group dynamics or interpersonal communications.

- Seek opportunities at the district and state levels to serve on committees.

- Participate in seminars dealing with effective management, administration, and meetings.

## Teamwork

- Conduct an assessment of the culture in your school or district to determine the atmosphere for risk-taking, meeting needs, and so on, and along with your team, develop a plan to improve the culture as needed. Understand that culture is nurtured, not discovered.

- Establish a group to be the "key communicators" within the school to solicit ideas, questions, and reactions to proposals. Make sure all stakeholder groups are represented, including teachers, other administrators, classified personnel, retired persons, business, students, and parents. Use this group to continually assess the needs of the diverse constituencies in your school community.

- When communicating expectations, be specific about the process or product. For example, when appointing a committee, indicate the task or purpose, timelines, and type of action needed.

- Practice working through people to help others get the job done. Participate in professional development activities that target teamwork, team building, and trust building. In addition to training activities, you might engage in self-directed learning such as maintaining a daily journal in which you note conversations and other interactions. At the end of each day, you can review your notes and reflect on how your words and actions were perceived by others. Such an analysis may indicate the need or desire for other development activities.

- To assist in resolving complex problems, begin with the end in mind. Read Stephen Covey's *The 7 Habits of Highly Effective People*, specifically Chapter 2, to gain a better understanding of who you are and the principles you use in achieving results in your work.

- Keep track of employees' other involvement, such as committees, and then add or rotate in new people or different people each time as you develop teams/committees.

- Challenge employees to bring a possible solution with every problem.

- Seek opportunities to serve on district and state level committees.

## Sensitivity

- Practice "active listening" in group settings. Make statements that indicate that you have heard correctly, understand, and respect the comments of others.

- Practice responding directly (in person, by phone, or in writing) to people who express needs, problems, or concerns.

- Have a trusted colleague read your correspondence and give you feedback regarding tone and sensitivity.

- Ask an administrative mentor or a trusted colleague for feedback regarding sensitivity expressed in group settings through verbal and nonverbal behaviors.

- Develop individual and school communication plans similar to your district's communication plan. Ensure that all affected staff members have copies of the necessary documents, letters, and other information. It is better to over-communicate than to under-communicate. Determine who in each area should receive what type of information. Regularly and systematically provide appropriate information to those people.

- Work with the principal or an administrative mentor to identify strategies for managing.

- Use the names of other group members as a means to draw them into the group activity and to show respect for the ideas of others.

- Observe an experienced colleague during the handling of a difficult or emotional conflict. Discuss the observation in terms of the sensitive behaviors that contributed to or hindered the successful resolution of the situation.

- Videotape or audiotape yourself participating in or leading a group meeting. Critique your sensitivity behavior alone or with the assistance of a colleague or mentor.

- To practice collecting behavioral data and giving feedback in a sensitive manner, serve as a peer coach to a trusted colleague.

- Practice delegating tasks that others in the group can successfully complete to increase their sense of belonging and accomplishment.

- Practice seeking input and advice from others. Incorporate appropriate advice into planning and decision making. Give appropriate credit to others for suggestions, advice, and assistance.

- Participate in interpersonal and communication skills development programs, workshops, and seminars.

- To become more aware of the needs, concerns, and problems of people from different backgrounds, volunteer to work in a community organization that serves the needs of people.

## Judgment

- Discuss the following with an administrative mentor:
    1. The kinds of school issues that need to be dealt with immediately
    2. Sensitive or potentially explosive situations and methods for handling them with caution
    3. Situations that require communication with central office personnel.

- Observe an experienced administrator as he or she attempts to address a critical problem or issue within the school. Discuss the observation with him or her to analyze the nature of the issue, the action taken, and the rationale for decisions made.

- For a period of time, analyze your information-seeking patterns. List the information pieces considered for each decision, then code each piece as essential, desirable but not essential, and irrelevant. Reflect on your findings to see if you are able to identify the information pieces you need and resist acquiring more than you need.

- Practice establishing priority rankings of the problems and issues facing the school or district and discuss this ranking with an administrative mentor.

- Work with an administrative mentor to analyze school-related problems (such as those related to assessment, discipline, school finance, students' and staff members' attendance, and scheduling) to identify relevant sources of information and assistance and to formulate strategies to seek solutions.

- Prior to making a decision, practice talking with individuals who will be affected by the decision to get additional information and different perspectives that may be critical to a more effective decision.

- Ask a trusted colleague to observe you in decision-making activities and give you feedback regarding your judgment as you make decisions. This might be a member of your staff who would frequently be included in situations where you are called upon to make decisions. Meet with the colleague weekly to assess your progress in avoiding premature decisions.

- Learn to ask at least three questions for clarification before making any decision. This provides wait time between facts and action.

- Seek other data sources that would assist in identifying problem areas. For example, discipline records (number of referrals, kind of referrals, from whom, etc.) demographic data. (Is the community stable? Does this diversity suggest changes in the curriculum or structure?) Seek individuals inside and outside the system who can help interpret the data.

- When presented with a situation (memo, phone call, verbal report, etc.) make a list of questions that would enable you to gather information needed to address the problem.

- Practice obtaining information from individuals presenting a problem as well as those affected by a problem, data in school and district files, survey instruments, experienced personnel, experts in a problem area, supervisors and mentors, and other sources specific to the situation.

- Select a problem. Gather relevant information from a variety of sources. Analyze the information collected. Write a proposal recommending strategies for solving the problem. Submit the proposal to appropriate personnel for consideration, feedback, and possible implementation. This might include the submission of a grant proposal.

- Participate in seminars that focus on the further development of judgment and problem analysis skills.

- Develop a mentor relationship with a trusted administrator who can provide guidance in identifying critical issues and in assigning appropriate priority to these issues.

- Serve on district-level committees, which seek solutions to critical issues within the district.

- Volunteer to serve on a regional accreditation team.
- Develop a mentor relationship with a trusted administrator who can provide guidance in and strategies for information gathering and analysis.

## Results Orientation

- Work with an administrative mentor to explore and analyze school situations in which immediate decisions or actions are required as well as school situations in which decisions or action may be delayed. Consider the appropriate actions needed and the priorities of various actions in response to specific situations.
- Explore and develop organizational techniques that incorporate setting priorities and timelines for actions or decisions.
- Discuss with an administrative mentor actual school issues focusing on the effective administrator's use of skills in problem analysis, judgment, organizational ability, and sensitivity in acting decisively.
- Seek committee leadership positions at the school or district levels.
- Observe a school administrator during the handling of a school crisis. When the issues are resolved, discuss with the administrator decisions made during the situation and the rationale for the decisions. Consider the long-term and short-term implications of the decision.
- Assist with the handling of a school crisis. When the issues are resolved, discuss with the administrative mentor the decisions made during the situation and the rationale for the decisions. Consider the skills of problem analysis, judgment, sensitivity, and organizational ability in the discussion.
- Participate in seminars, programs, or workshops designed to develop skill in making effective decisions.

## Organizational Ability

- Discuss with an administrative mentor organizational techniques he or she has found to be effective in handling many complex details while maintaining a realistic perception of the "big picture."
- Work with an administrative mentor to explore and develop techniques for completing multiple tasks in a timely manner.
- Practice using calendars, to-do-lists, and action plans for organizing work, setting priorities, and managing complex responsibilities. Investigate the use of technology to work with calendars, to-do-lists, etc.
- Develop and use time-lines for the completion of multiple or complex tasks.
- Discuss with the administrative mentor the conditions and strategies for delegating tasks.
- Seek leadership responsibility for groups assigned to accomplish specific tasks. Practice delegating tasks and responsibilities to group members. Develop procedures for monitoring work delegated and for providing feedback.
- Develop priority task lists with subordinates. Manage your tasks and those of others by setting objectives and prioritizing them in terms of time and importance.

- Evaluate your office organization focusing on provision of opportunity for each individual to contribute to the success of the organization.
- Practice using a personal planning calendar. Practice setting deadlines for yourself and your staff. Use a "tickler file" to check your progress and the progress of others in meeting expectations and deadlines.
- Construct a decision-making timeline for the fiscal year specifying all major decisions that need to be made, the information needed for those decisions, the parties responsible for making the final decision.
- Develop a mentor relationship with a trusted administrator who is known to be strong in organizational ability.
- Participate in a workshop or seminar on strategic planning.
- Participate in a seminar dealing with effective management practices, time management, or administrative effectiveness.

## Oral Communication

- Make presentations to groups within the school and district as frequently as possible. Ask an administrative mentor or trusted colleague to give you feedback regarding voice quality (tone, volume, rate of speaking, and clarity), use of appropriate presentation devices (organization of thoughts, use of visual aids, use of organizers, vocal inflection, use of correct grammar and pronunciation, use of gestures and positive body language, and appropriate eye contact), and the content of the presentation.
- Videotape some of the presentations you make and evaluate them for oral communication effectiveness. Ask a mentor or colleague to assist you in your evaluation.
- Practice organizing thoughts so that comments are concise and easily followed by the listener.
- Ask a mentor or trusted colleague for feedback regarding organization of thoughts in impromptu oral presentations.
- Solicit feedback on the clarity and thoroughness of your oral communications.
- Develop notes or an outline to assist in organization of thoughts during presentations to groups.
- Join Toastmasters or a similar organization that promotes the development of public speaking skills.
- Participate in programs, workshops, and seminars designed to develop skills in effective oral communication and public speaking.
- Seek opportunities to practice effective oral communication skills by making presentations to community groups, professional associations, and other groups.

## Written Communication

- Use a dictionary, style manual, and thesaurus when writing documents to be read by others.
- Practice proofreading all documents you write to ensure that written communication is composed of well-developed paragraphs and is free of errors.

- Establish a "buddy system" with a trusted colleague to ensure that correspondence is proofread prior to transmittal.
- Volunteer to prepare press releases, news bulletins, program descriptions, grant proposals, and other documents for the school or district. Seek feedback from a mentor or trusted colleague regarding correctness and effectiveness of written communication.
- Secure and develop skill in the use of a word processing program that provides spelling and grammar checks.
- Participate in programs, workshops, and seminars designed to develop skill in effective business and technical writing.

## Developing Others

- Practice communicating personal educational values to others in both written and oral forms. Seek feedback from a mentor or colleague regarding the communication of educational values in correspondence and other written material.
- Seek feedback from staff as to the value of support they have received in designing and evaluating their professional development plan.
- Work with a mentor or colleague who is skilled in designing strategies for motivating staff to improve instructional effectiveness.
- Discuss with colleagues ways to model change for your staff.
- Organize a study group to focus on an area that you have identified as a need for additional professional development. Invite two or three others on your staff to join you in an in-depth study of this concern. Meet regularly to share ideas and concepts gained from your reading or investigation.
- Practice making behaviorally specific notes while observing an individual or group. Deliver the feedback, focusing on behavior demonstrated.
- Identify the 20% of employees who are initiators and innovators. Give them opportunities (both large and small) to be leaders
- Practice identifying the strengths of others. Assign or delegate to them tasks that develop those strengths.
- Make a list of major activities, such as SIC, PTO, Strategic Planning, Booster Club, etc. Identify cochairpersons or assistant group leaders who are staff members to assume responsibility for the task under your leadership.
- Develop a rotating leadership team for your school (department chairpersons or grade level chairs) that meets regularly to address issues, to provide communication from specific areas of campus, and to provide feedback to the principal.
- Participate in programs, workshops, and seminars designed to build skill in observing behavior and delivering feedback to others.
- Serve as a mentor to new teachers in a teacher induction program.
- Volunteer to develop or assist in developing a leadership training program for your district.

Appendix 6
Developmental Strategies

## Understanding Your Own Strengths & Weaknesses

■ Develop a mentor relationship with a trusted colleague who is highly motivated. Review personal career goals with the mentor. Discuss the development or the refinement of short-range and long-range career goals and an accompanying career development plan.

■ Discuss with a mentor or colleague techniques used to effectively cope with stress.

■ Engage in dialogue with a mentor or colleague and other experienced educators to more clearly define your personal educational value system.

■ Practice communicating personal educational values and professional strength to others in both written and oral forms. Seek feedback from a mentor or colleague or trusted professional colleagues regarding the communication.

■ Make a chart of your educational/professional goals. Ask, "Where do I want to be and when?" Develop an action plan to accomplish your goals. Periodically review your goals statements and action plans, and reflect on your progress. Revise as necessary.

■ Read *Beyond Ambition*, by Robert E. Kaplan. This book is based on an intensive six-year study of senior executives whose drive to excel was actually damaging their performance. It reveals how managers can recognize and change personality traits (perfectionism or the need to over-control) that undermine effectiveness.

■ Attend to your mental and physical health. Plan to do something that you enjoy and that provides physical exercise.

■ Participate in seminars or workshops that are designed to help participants better understand their leadership profile.

■ Update your skills in technology. Expand your current understanding to become knowledgeable about and proficient in applications to curriculum and instructional practices.

■ Spend time with your mentor. Develop a network of peers in your area made up of some who are at your same level of experience, some who have more experience than you, and some who have less experience than you. This will provide a support group for sharing concerns and successes and a means for becoming more knowledgeable about a wide variety of school issues.

■ Create a network with several other educational leaders in your area to serve as a learning community for you. Meet periodically with network members to share problems and potential solutions to those problems.

■ Work with a mentor or colleague, family members, and possibly your doctor to assess the work, family, social, physical, and emotional demands on you. Develop strategies and action plans to maintain balance between time and energy directed at meeting the complex demands on a school administrator.

■ Become more actively involved in the work of the professional associations of which you are a member.

■ Read the journals of professional associations and periodicals. Discuss your reading with your mentor or colleagues.

- Seek opportunities to chair problem-solving committees at the school level. Ask a mentor or colleague to monitor progress and provide feedback regarding effective use of planning skills and follow-through.
- Seek opportunities to serve on district or state level problem-solving committees.
- Seek opportunities to work with others in developing departmental, school, district, or organizational mission statements.
- Participate in activities like a critical issue forum at district, state, regional, or national levels.
- Participate in career planning programs, workshops, and seminars.
- Establish a monthly pattern of reading one or two books or articles in professional areas other than education.
- Regularly read professional journals to develop broader knowledge and understanding of educational issues. Formulate and communicate orally and in writing clear statements of your position relative to these issues.

Appendix 6
Developmental Strategies